Nietzsche on Dithyrambic Music

NIETZSCHE ON DITHYRAMBIC MUSIC
A Reiteration of *Richard Wagner in Bayreuth*

by

James Chester

JAMES CHESTER PUBLISHING

Copyright © 2021 James Chester

All rights reserved. No part of this publication may be reproduced, distributed, or transmitted in any form or by any means, including photocopying, recording, or other electronic or mechanical methods, without the prior written permission of the publisher, except in the case of brief quotations embodied in reviews and certain other non-commercial uses permitted by copyright law. For permission requests, contact the publisher at the address below.

Published in the United States by James Chester Publishing, Boston, Massachusetts
All inquiries may be made at www.JamesChester.org.

Library of Congress Control Number: 2021910446
ISBN: 978-1-7350167-5-7 (paperback)

First edition 2021.
Front cover image by Rembrandt van Rijn, Return of the Prodigal Son, c. 1661-1669.

Book design by James Chester.

Printed in the United States of America

FOR THE PHILOSOPHER — AND HIS PUPIL

Table of Contents

PREFACE 13
CHAPTER 1 1

Genius in a Vision 1
Genius in a Will to Self.. 1
The Discovery of the Supra-Conscious 2
Genius in a Map of an Inner Journey..................................... 3
Tragedy as Proto-Tragedy.. 3
Nietzsche Chooses His Audience as a Precaution 4
Gesticulative Metaphor as a Cloak and a Pointer 6
Dithyrambic Drama and Endurance 7
Upon Discovering the Passion in Dithyrambic Music 10
Dithyrambic Drama *Only* in the Future 10
Dithyrambic Drama as Art in the Creation of Myth.............. 12
The Failure of Dithyrambic Art in "Modern" Times............... 14

CHAPTER 2 17

Dithyrambic Drama as the Will to Power 19
Dithyrambic Drama as Physician 20
Dithyrambic Drama Applies to Everyone Universally........... 23
"Thus Spoke Zarathustra" Means "Thus Spoke the Will to Power" 23
Out of Chaos, A "Musical" Will Emerges 25
The Dithyramb as a Universally Applicable Personal Testimonial 25
The Dithyramb and Self 27

CHAPTER 3 31

The Dithyramb and Mysticism.. 31
Self, Supra-Self, and Over-Self.. 32
Self as Mediator to the Apollonian-Dionysian duality.......... 33
The Practice of Dithyrambic Drama Requires Leisure 34

Tragedy Invokes Nausea with Life 35
    Nietzsche's Music is the Subject of *Richard Wagner in Bayreuth* 36
The Fundaments of Will: Desire, Hope, and Belief 37
Metaphor Made Articulation Easy for Nietzsche 40
"Noontide" as a Metaphor 40
    A Process of Inner Growth that is Never-ending and Leads to a Grand Hope 41
Will as Cultivation, not Frenzy 44
The Dithyrambic Actor Becomes Himself a Work of Art 46
The Dithyramb is Encrypted 47
Art as a Gateway to Culture 47
The Dithyrambist as Myth Maker and Poet 49
Myth Empowers the Will 50
The Poignancy of Dithyrambic Poetry 51
Dead Myth as a Desperate Lifeline 52

CHAPTER 4 55

Dithyrambic Drama as Cultural Physician 55
Dithyrambic Tragedy as Life's Most Valuable Asset 58
A Definition of Art 61
Art in the Will as Idea 62
Love of Myth and Life 63
Art as the Creation of Genius 64
Art as Justice in Life 66
Life is not Possible without Tragedy 67
Actuality versus Reality 68

CHAPTER 5 71

Dithyrambic Drama as a Simplification of the World 71
Dithyrambic Drama as the Will to Power 72
Dithyrambic Drama as a True Depiction of Reality 73
Dithyrambic Drama as Instruction via Feeling, not Concept . 73
The Dithyrambist Creates Will with Embodiable Passions 75
The Birth of a New Culture via Dithyrambic Drama 76
Dithyrambic Music and Love of Nature 78

Art as Passion and Vision 79
The Town Called "The Pied Cow" or "The Motley Cow" 79
Ego Precludes the Practice of Dithyrambic Drama; It Requires Self 84
A Definition of Dithyrambic Music 85
Transformative Art Will Also Transform Society 89
Dithyrambic Drama is not Entertainment 90
Modern Art Has No Depth, but Dithyrambic Drama Runs Very Deep 91
Modern Man and the Fear of Self 93

CHAPTER 6 95

A Critique of Modern Values 95
The Pursuit of Self Requires a Protracted and Discerning Effort 97
Art Heals the Bad Conscience 100
Nietzsche's Invention of the Dithyramb 101
Dithyrambic Drama Requires Mystery and Defies Logic 105
Music as Will to Self and Power 107
Dithyrambic Music and Human Nature 111

CHAPTER 7 113

Dithyrambic Drama as Transport into the Soul of the Dithyrambist 113
"Music" and Appearance as Emotion and Self 116
Dithyrambic Drama as Music, Poetry, and Acting 117
The Dithyrambist as Primordial Artist of Actuality 119
Self as Mediator and Governor 120
Actuality as a Repudiation of Reality 121
Fear of the Power of the Dithyramb 123
The Dithyramb Does Not Speak to Idealism, only Actuality 123
The Dithyramb as Healer to Suffering Man 124
Will as Evaluator of Emotion 125
The Value of Tragedy to Life 126
The Dithyrambic Actor as Tragic Hero 126

Tragedy as a Danger to Life that Cures Itself 128
The Birth of Tragedy Out of Dissonance 129
The Will as Music 130
Tragedy as Love of Human Nature 132
Tragedy Effects Clairvoyance into Human Nature 133
Love of Self as Will to Power 135
Nietzsche's Theory of the Origin of Things in Their Opposite
.... 136
The Tragic Incorporation of Dismembered Emotion into Self
Provides Profound Catharsis 137
Mystery is Another Fundamental Component of Tragedy .. 141
Summation of Nietzsche's Theory of the Origin of Things in
their Opposite 142
The Dithyramb as a Language of Feeling, Not Concept 144
Emotion Arises from within Actuality and Reality Arises from
within Self 144
Will as Dithyrambic Music 145
Self as Image of Nature and as Healer with Illusion 147
Mythical Self as Tragic Hero 148
Being as a Dangerous Satiety of the Will 149
Tragedy as Dissonance Cures Satiety of the Will 150
Genius as the Goal of Life 150
Dithyrambic Drama as Teacher of Tragic Thought and Invoker
of Mythopoeia 151
The Condensation of Supra-Self into Existing Self 152

CHAPTER 8 155

Dithyrambic Drama Chooses Its Audience 156
Love of Self Equates to Love of Emotions 157
The Naturalization of Man 158
Dithyrambic Music as Melos 159
Life as the Will to Power 161
The Psychology of Self Becomes the Mythopoeia of Self 162
Dead Myth Versus Living Myth 163
Genius in the Restoration of Myth 164
Myth as the Middle Ground 165
Dithyrambic Myth is Natural 165
A Radical Departure from Traditional Form 167

CHAPTER 9 169

The Dithyramb as Real Experience 169
The Multiple Talents of the Dithyramb 170
Mythical Thought Is Not Conceptual Thought..................... 172
Is Not Founded on a Single Thought.................................... 174
Myth is Founded in Feelings 176
Explaining the Dithyramb and Living the Dithyramb........... 177
The Dithyrambic Drama Blocks Entrance to Theoretical Man
 178
Dithyrambic Drama Requires Initiation 179
Tragedy as Naïve Mysticism 180
Dithyrambic Transport as Teacher 182
Dithyrambic Drama and Poetry 183
Dithyrambic Drama as Cultivation of the Will 185
On the Poignancy of the Dithyramb 186
The Dithyramb is Transformative and Redemptive............. 188
The Dithyramb and the Over-Self, the Übermensch 190

CHAPTER 10 191

Insights into the Legacy of Dithyrambic Drama................... 192
The Dithyrambic Actor Becomes a Work of Art 193
The Dithyramb Teaches Instinct 194

CHAPTER 11 197

True Freedom Comes from Within....................................... 197
The Reason We Suffer 198
A Natural and an Unnatural Way of Life.............................. 198
Morality Versus Tragedy as a Way of Life 199
A Definition of Morality... 200
A Condemnation of Morality 201
The Will Wants Becoming, Not Being................................... 202
Nietzsche's Legacy: The Birth of Dionysia 202

IN SUMMARY 205

Preface

What I am about to reveal in the following reiteration of *Richard Wagner in Bayreuth* is Nietzsche's vision of the new dithyramb *in its latency*. While it had clearly developed into an advanced form at the time Nietzsche wrote this essay, it had not yet entered into his consciousness and his will. Consequently, when he speaks of it, he speaks of it only via a projection onto that which he admires, which in this case is Richard Wagner and Wagner's music. And what he indirectly reveals in that projection is his aborning knowledge of dithyrambic music and *Thus Spoke Zarathustra* as a dithyrambic tragedy.

To speak of dithyrambic music is to speak of something that Nietzsche re-invented, and it is important to understand what it is because the text in which *Thus Spoke Zarathustra* is written is, in fact, a composition of dithyrambic music, not a story, or an allegory, or anything else with which we are already familiar. Dithyrambic drama is something entirely new. And its power to draw its audience into itself so that they begin acting out the drama *themselves* brilliantly *defies* our present-day notion of drama or *any other* existing art form.

Dithyrambic music has otherwise never existed in

modern times, though Nietzsche claims that some composers in ancient times perfected it, and some modern composers have dabbled in it here and there, though probably unawares. The only nearest existent is lyrical poetry, but dithyrambic music is much more than mere lyrical poetry. While expressive lyrical writing has always been a literary representation of a state of mind arising out of a passion, which it *described*, dithyrambic music is a literary representation of a state of mind arising out of *will*, which it *evokes*. The experience that an individual undergoes in the course of reading the most beautiful lyrical poem is very different from the experience he has while listening to the most moving traditional audible music. And that is the difference between lyrical poetry and dithyrambic poetry. Dithyrambic music moves the listener with emotion as obviously as does traditional music. The comparisons between dithyrambic music, as a literary representation of the will, and traditional, audible music are replete throughout this essay.

However, it is not necessary, for the sake of this reiteration, to understand dithyrambic music as a literary representation to the point of being able to read it; it is only necessary to understand that it is a new form of drama so that an education in its practice can begin.

And finally, insofar as Nietzsche wrote this essay not as a disquisition on the dithyramb but rather as a glowing adoration of Wagner's music, the order of his revelations is rather haphazard, which means we will be jumping from one point to another with little or no cohesion in between. Nonetheless, the insights into his *Thus Spoke Zarathustra* are most valuable.

This reiteration is not intended as an introduction of any kind to Nietzsche's work. On the contrary, it will most likely be understood and helpful only to those readers who have already become familiar with the dithyramb and dithyrambic music after having read my other books, *The Birth of Dionysia* and *Dionysia Metaphysica*.

Nor is it my intent to put forth any arguments with this reiteration. With my first two books, I have already documented Nietzsche's creation of dithyrambic music and dithyrambic drama and his theories of proto-tragedy and life as art and will to Self or power. I simply want to present my reading of *Richard Wagner in Bayreuth*, which is very different from what Nietzsche actually wrote but spot-on for what he meant.

Lastly, I should warn you that the insights flow like a dribble, slowly at first and seemingly trivial if not boring, but they eventually yield gems, like the one that shows the kernel of thought out of which Nietzsche crystallized his theory of dithyrambic music.

In the end, I believe the reader will understand much more of what Nietzsche said in *Richard Wagner in Bayreuth* than he would understand otherwise without this reiteration.

Chapter 1

Genius in a Vision

One of the most prominent traits of genius is a vision of something in the future to which the beholden individual strives in order to create it and make it happen. And it is a peculiar thing how that vision grips the beholden individual at an early age, in his young twenties, sometimes sooner, and drives him unawares. It is only later in life that the vision crystallizes and enters his consciousness in an overt form. In Nietzsche's case, the vision was the founding of a new culture, a new way of thinking, that healed suffering man and rendered his suffering both meaningful and worthwhile.

Genius in a Will to Self

Concurrent with his innate striving toward the founding of a new culture, Nietzsche was being driven by a will within himself into his own subliminal suffering, which lay hidden and inaccessible to him within his subconscious. That will to plumb his subconscious, as it turned out, generated a simultaneous and symbiotic will toward a vision of his Self. And that twofold will was his second, equally prodigious genius. And it gripped him very early on. In his essay *On Moods*, which he wrote when he was only nineteen years old, we clearly see evidence of it.

> That which is now perhaps your whole happiness or your whole heartache will perhaps in a short time be only the garment of an even deeper feeling, and will therefore disappear in itself when the higher [passion] comes. And so, our moods deepen more and more; not one is exactly like another, but each is unfathomably young and the birth of the moment.[1]

The Discovery of the Supra-Conscious

The reader must look very closely at those written words to see my point. If you do, you will see a tendency to look beyond the surface of things and more deeply into an underlying essence. And that tendency plays significantly in the rendition of dithyrambic music. Beyond that, his statement also evinces a tendency to seek feelings that are deeper than those that already exist. And those abilities, to look beyond the surface of things and more deeply into an underlying essence and to look for

---

[1] Friedrich Nietzsche: *Werke in drei Bänden. Band 3*, Herausgegeben von Karl Schlechta. München: Hanser, 1954, pp. 113-116.

deeper feelings beyond moods, which is uncommon among men, played out critically in Nietzsche's genius. It drove him ever more deeply into his own subconscious, wherein he found his Self and his demons, struggled to free himself from their grip, and, in his success, ascended into the supra-conscious, which he singlehandedly discovered, wherein all his suffering was redeemed and made worthwhile.

> ... I had undertaken something which could not have been done by everybody: I went down into the deepest depths [of the subconscious]; I tunneled to the very bottom [of the subconscious] ....[2]

Genius in a Map of an Inner Journey

Beyond navigating and successfully completing that very difficult journey, it then behooved him to chart it for others. And to do that, he created an entirely new form of drama called the New Dithyramb. I say "new" because Nietzsche claimed to have reclaimed it from antiquity, specifically Greek antiquity, from the time in their history when they began celebrating the destruction of magnificent individuality with their tragic dramas.

Tragedy as Proto-Tragedy

Coincidentally, during his journey to his innermost Self, Nietzsche, too, experienced something like a

---

[2] Nietzsche, Friedrich. *The Dawn of Day*. Translated by John M. Kennedy, London: George Allen & Unwin LTD, 1911, p. 2.

tragedy. He discovered that a true apprehension of one's innermost Self requires letting go of one's Ego, letting it die out or "go under." And that inner rite of passage is one of the major events that he charted into his map. In fact, he identified it as the original form of tragedy, proto-tragedy, before it transformed into the modern theatrical tragedies with which we are so familiar today. Thus, the new dithyrambic drama he created as a map of his journey is a dithyrambic tragedy.

Nietzsche Chooses His Audience as a Precaution

The charting of Nietzsche's proto-tragic sojourn into the subconscious and his subsequent redemptive ascension into the supra-conscious — and the novel way of thinking that drove and sustained it — is Nietzsche's paramount achievement, a great event, a milestone in the course of the history of Western civilization. Upon its creation, his next big step would determine whether his success prevailed by impressing itself upon humanity or whether it faded forever into oblivion.

> For an event to have greatness, two things must come together: the great sense of those who accomplish it and the great sense of those who experience it. No event in itself has greatness, and when whole constellations disappear, peoples perish, vast states are founded, and wars are fought with enormous forces and losses, the breath of history blows over many of them as if they were flakes. But it also happens that a

mighty man strikes a blow that sinks ineffectually on a hard rock; a brief sharp echo, and all is over. History knows almost nothing to report even of such blunt events. So, everyone who sees an event approaching is overcome by the worry whether those who experience it will be worthy of it. Whenever one acts, one counts on and aims at this correspondence between action and receptivity, in the smallest as well as in the greatest; and he who wants to give must see to it that he finds the takers who will do enough for the purpose of his gift. For this very reason even the single act of a man, even a great one, has no greatness if it is short, dull, and barren; for at the very moment he did it he must have lacked the profound insight that it was necessary at this very moment: he had not aimed sharply enough, had not recognized and chosen the time with sufficient determination: chance had become master of him, while being great and having an eye for necessity belonged together strictly.

- "For an event to have greatness, two things must come together: the great sense of those who accomplish it and the great sense of those who experience it."

CHAPTER 1

According to this, Nietzsche required that the individual who would undertake the journey he mapped out in *Thus Spoke Zarathustra* should possess uncommon ability. At the very least, as we have already discussed, the individual must possess the ability to look beyond the surface of things, beyond the horizon of percipience, and this is especially obvious when you consider the difficulty involved in looking beyond one's feelings for deeper feelings and the tendency to be drawn tightly round the horizon imposed by a sense of Self.

Gesticulative Metaphor as a Cloak and a Pointer

To that end, the composition in metaphor provides the dithyramb a two-fold advantage. First, it steers away those readers who are disinclined to look more deeply into the meaning of things. But more importantly, it provides a language of *gestures* that is absent any reference whatsoever to concept as well as any existent within the temporal world. And if the words are absent any reference to the physical world, any physically existing thing, or even concept, what, then, do the words point to? They point to *feelings*, which exist only within the reader, nowhere else. Lyrical poetry also uses words to denote feelings in the way that the phrase "angry man" will prompt the reader to *conceptualize* an angry man. And that is the difference. Dithyrambic poetry does not denote anything that is meant to be conceptualized. Instead, the use of metaphor in dithyrambic poetry is meant to lead the reader into a specific mood arising out of a specific feeling. In other words, the reader must embody, not conceptualize, the feeling that the metaphor denotes. It is not a concept that the reader must reach for while reading dithyrambic poetry; what he must reach for is a feeling —

and then literally enter into the feeling. Embodiment is the key activity in dithyrambic poetry, not conceptualization, and it is embodiment that transforms dithyrambic poetry into dithyrambic drama, which also transforms the reader from observer and spectator into actor and participant.

But given the metaphors in which the dithyrambs are composed, a cursory reading, which would necessarily be absent those feelings, easily indicates a story about a character named Zarathustra and his travels around a town called the Motley Cow. But there is no town called the Motley Cow, and there is no character named Zarathustra. Nor is there even a story.

Thus, a reading of *Thus Spoke Zarathustra* requires an ability to look beyond the surface of things. Without the ability to look beyond the horizon, an individual would not be able to sense the supra-Self in his subliminal feelings, nor would he be able to eventually come upon the over-Self, and creation of the over-Self is the whole point of the drama.

Dithyrambic Drama and Endurance

But there are other traits in addition to the ability to look beyond the horizon that also play a critical role in the completion of the drama. Endurance is high on the list. The journey into the subconscious is a protracted one that is defined by numerous severe obstacles that require, on the one hand, extended waiting time for the mood that should fill the sails of the will to drive it forward and, on the other, the summoning of unusual and mighty passions to bolster the will. Plus, there are many paths to learn, which requires first finding the junctions, or circumstances of emotion and conscience, out of which

Chapter 1

those paths originate. All of these obstacles require endurance: the ability to keep in sight the vision toward which one strives as well as the muster of passions that comprise the will upon which the journey proceeds, or at least the stamina to summon those passions opportunely.

- "But it also happens that a mighty man strikes a blow that sinks ineffectually on a hard rock; a brief sharp echo, and all is over."

Thus, we may say that Nietzsche was a great man, insofar as he journeyed to the bottom of the earth, the subconscious, which no one else had ever done. And then, beyond that, he discovered the supra-conscious, as the consummation of the journey, which, again, no one else had ever discovered. And finally, as his crowning achievement, he mapped out the entire journey, with all its twists and turns, thereby enabling others after him to undertake the journey themselves. Therefore, if this is true, what I say he achieved, then we might reconsider his assertion that, with *Thus Spoke Zarathustra,* he has given mankind its "greatest gift, as being spot on and not the trivial utterance of an egomaniac, as some have speculated.

However, it is also possible, especially given the false countenance of a story that *Thus Spoke Zarathustra* presents, that he may have struck a blow that sinks ineffectually and "all is over."

- "So, everyone who sees an event approaching is overcome by the worry whether those who experience it will be worthy of it."

Given the risks that Nietzsche understood he was

taking with his great book, he also understood that his mighty strike might sink ineffectually into oblivion, and he had to take measures to prevent that from happening. It is my belief that his writing in metaphor, which came to him naturally, given his philosophical nature, provided that safeguard. As it turns out, however, the metaphorical composition provided much more than mere safeguard, insofar as it became the essence of dithyrambic music with its gesticulative reference to passion absent any concept whatsoever, so that the reader enters a world comprised entirely of emotion and utterly absent a single, simple concept, which is unlike anything that the reader, whoever he is, has ever read before.

> In Bayreuth the spectator is also worth watching, there is no doubt about it. A wiser contemplating mind, which would go from one century to the next to compare the strange cultural movements, would have much to see there; he would have to feel that he suddenly finds himself in warm waters here, like one who swims in a lake and comes close to the current of a hot spring: for other, deeper reasons it must rise, he tells himself, the surrounding water does not explain it and is in any case itself of shallower origin.

Please remember my earlier admonition that the insights I draw out of Nietzsche's writing in this essay may appear haphazard or lacking a cohesion and that is because he was painting his image of Wagner, which was really a vision of himself, as he admitted in Ecco Homo, while at the same time unknowingly revealing the vision of his genius in that image, with that vision being dithyrambic music.

Upon Discovering the Passion in Dithyrambic Music

- "…like one who swims in a lake and comes close to the current of a hot spring."

And in this comment, he reveals the experience one has upon looking beyond the metaphors in which the dithyramb is composed and discovering the will within the representation: "he suddenly finds himself in warm waters here … the surrounding waters [metaphors, and the false countenance of a story] does not explain it and is in any case itself of shallower origin." In other words, if you read the text in which *Thus Spoke Zarathustra* is composed literally, there is no depth in what you find, compared to reading the text as gesticulative metaphors that point to passions you can find within yourself and provide significant depth.

Dithyrambic Drama *Only* in the Future

> Thus, all those who celebrate the Bayreuth Festival will be perceived as outmoded people: they have their home elsewhere than in time and find elsewhere both their explanation and their justification.

Regarding the phrase "outmoded people," the

German reads as "unzeitgemäße Menschen" and "unzeitgemäße" translates as not just "outmoded" but also "unseasonable," "untimely," and "inopportune." And I would choose "untimely" as the use Nietzsche intended in the above statement.

This is just one of many times when Nietzsche mentions the fact that he does not believe people in his time will understand *Thus Spoke Zarathustra* and that it will be a very long time before someone succeeds in understanding it. Exactly what it is that would prevent existing people from understanding his dithyrambic tragedy, even if they knew how to render the metaphors, is not entirely clear, but he mentions current times not being sufficiently hard enough on people to produce individuals with the strength that is needed to undertake the journey.

And for the same reasons, anyone who does succeed in understanding it — and experiencing it — would also not be understood by their contemporaries and would find "their explanation and their justification" only in another, future time.

Moreover, and perhaps as a result of that future explanation and justification finally coming to the fore, other less inclined and less qualified individuals would finally partake in the experience that dithyrambic drama offers but not before. And if that is the case, then it might rightly be said that *Thus Spoke Zarathustra* was written for a people that did not yet exist (in the late 19th century, or even in the twentieth century). Indeed, that is precisely what happened. It wasn't until the year 2020 in the twenty-first century that someone finally spoke of a true experience of *Thus Spoke Zarathustra*, which followed a

Chapter 1

passage of one-hundred and thirty-seven years after its publication.

> The fact that a single person, in the course of an ordinary human life, could add something quite new, may outrage all those who swear by the gradualness of all development as if it were a kind of moral law: they themselves are slow and demand slowness - and here they see a very rapidity, do not know how he does it ....

It may be difficult for some people to fathom the invention of an entirely new art form in the course of a single lifespan. And if that is the case, if the reader cannot simply allow for the possible emergence of something unheard of and entirely new, the difficulty will only add resistance to that person's willingness to accept and embrace this invention. To those people, I would advise that they consider Nietzsche's genius.

Dithyrambic Drama as Art in the Creation of Myth

> There were no omens, no transitions, no mediations from such an undertaking as the Bayreuth one; the long way to the goal and the goal itself was known only to Wagner. It is the first circumnavigation of the world in the realm of art: whereby, as it seems, not only a new art, but art itself was

> discovered. All the modern arts up to now have been half and half devalued by this, as hermit-like, stunted or as luxury arts; even the uncertain, badly connected memories of a true art, which we newcomers had from the Greeks, may now rest, in so far as they cannot shine in a new understanding even now. Now is the time for many things to die; this new art is a seer who sees the decline approaching not only for the arts. Her admonishing hand must seem very uncanny to our whole present education from the moment when the laughter at her parodies ceases ….

- "… not only a new art, but art itself was discovered."

He makes several points here. He says that the invention of a new art form in the dithyramb represented something much more significant than just that and claims that art itself was discovered in the process. He is referring to mythopoeia, the creation of myth, as the highest manifestation of art in life, by which I mean the creation of something that is both beautiful and powerful out of sheer nothingness. And when you look at the numerous, highly defined "movements" of will that are depicted in each of the dithyrambs and how those movements add to a will out of which mythopoeia occurs, with that, Nietzsche rightly proclaims this is how art is done. In comparison, the so-called creations of art all around us in

CHAPTER 1

"cultivated" society pale in the paucity of reality and meaning in their character. There really is no comparison between dithyrambic drama and, say, Beethoven's ninth symphony, for which I have the highest esteem, or a Shakespearean tragedy, especially if you deem art's ability to draw you in as an accurate earmark of good art. And that is because dithyrambic drama requires embodiment of the "music," the will, which then converts the reader into an actor as he or she becomes driven by the will through the journey into the subconscious and then beyond into the supra-conscious. In such a way, the reader, as actor, himself becomes a work of art. Thus, there is no greater experience of art than that offered by dithyrambic drama. And the comparison of this particular potency enfeebles all that we have previously known of art in literature, music, and drama.

The Failure of Dithyrambic Art in "Modern" Times

When he speaks of his new invention being parodied, he postulates that the difficulties inherent in its comprehension and appreciation as well as its sudden appearance in this world may lead to it being mocked. And he says that only when the parodies end will people finally understand the power of the dithyramb and understand how it is a model for true creativity next to which conventional creativity will appear diminished as weak. However, I have seen no mockery of *Thus Spoke Zarathustra*, though I have seen occasional dismissiveness. By and large, people have respected Nietzsche's invention as a monumental enigma. The most major problem with people understanding the drama has been the universally adopted proposition that it tells a story or presents an allegory. The failure to see it as a composition of dithyrambic music and dithyrambic poetry that requires embodiment and enactment as a dithyrambic drama has been the single most difficult obstacle to its success.

Chapter 2

Now he begins to reveal things, though we could hardly say that his writing is revealing without first reiterating it.

> It would be strange if what a man does best and loves to do best were not also to become visible again in the whole organization of his life; rather, in people of outstanding ability, as in everyone, life must become not only a reflection of character, but above all a reflection of the intellect and of his own ability. The life of the epic poet will carry something of the epic in itself - as is incidentally the case with Goethe, in whom the Germans are very wrongly accustomed to see the poet in particular - the life of the dramatist will be dramatic.

In other words, we expect to see something of a man's abilities and his inclinations in his history and especially in what he has become at the end of life. A man with an inclination to accumulate wealth should have some measure of wealth at the end of his life *if* he also

CHAPTER 2

possessed the ability to accumulate wealth. Then Nietzsche says that a man with the ability and the inclination to compose drama should have a drama to tell at the end of his life.

And what was the drama in which Nietzsche became embroiled in his lifetime? He is now going to tell us, but you will never understand what he says in the following passage because he writes so vaguely and in such very generalized terms. How he ever expected *anyone* to understand *anything* when he wrote in his very indefinite and unclear manner is quite beyond me. The only reason I am able to understand is because I relived his soul by learning to read his dithyrambic music and practice his dithyrambic drama. Thus, I am able to see as if through glasses that no one else possesses. And that is the only reason I am able to understand.

> The dramatic in Wagner's *development* cannot be misjudged from the moment when the passion that reigns within him becomes conscious of itself and sums up his entire nature: with it the groping, the wandering, the proliferation of the side-shoots is done away with, and in the most intricate paths and changes, in the often-adventurous bowing of his plans, a single inner lawfulness prevails, a will from which they can be explained

The drama in Nietzsche's life is very defined and very clear after that point, which I would guess is about twenty years old, when "the passion that reigns within him becomes conscious of itself." And that passion is a passion to fathom the depths of his subconscious wherein lie the most horrific and most titanic emotions that an individual can experience, whatever those emotions are, though I would put forth the argument that they are most commonly humiliation, fear, and pain.

And the reason I speculate as I do about the nature of this passion is because (1) that is what his drama is all about, according to my experience, which, again, is fifty years long, and (2) that is the passion that begins to dawn upon him at the age of nineteen, according to what he wrote in his brief essay, *On Moods*, as I documented in *The Birth of Dionysia*, and (3) that is what he states, *outright*, almost twenty years later in the preface to *The Dawn*.[3]

Dithyrambic Drama as the Will to Power

Lastly, he states that, after plumbing his depths, a "single inner lawfulness prevailed" within him, "a will" through which the "most intricate paths and changes" within him "can be explained." That will is the will to power. And it does not derive solely from emotional elements but as well from the cerebral elements that arise from out of mythical Self.

> As soon as his spiritual and moral manhood comes into being, the drama of his life begins. And how different the sight is now! His nature appears

---

[3] Ibid.

> terribly simplified, torn apart into two drives or spheres.

In the depths of the subconscious, Nietzsche discovered not only the power of the realm of sensations, which he called the Dionysian realm, but also the power of Self and the gradations arising out of its growth, which he called the Apollonian realm and which increased in brilliance in direct proportion as the intensity of his emotions increased, as he brought the subconscious into consciousness. And out of that symbiosis, he experienced increasing empowerment and discovered the will to power. And all the inner world became interpretable in reference to the will to power. He had discovered the primary motivation in *all* human behavior, if you can believe that is a possibility.

> At the bottom [of his nature] a fierce will burrows in a sudden current, which, as it were, wants to come to light on all paths, caves and ravines and demands power.

Dithyrambic Drama as Physician

The will that "burrows" and "demands power" is the will to power plumbing the depths of the subconscious and then celebrating its success in the heights of ideational reflections that arise as a redemptive counterpart to those depths *and its horror*. This is the meaning of his analogy, which he stated in *The Birth of Tragedy*, of someone looking directly into the sun and then seeing dark spots as a remedy when he finally looks away except in the opposite sense, wherein someone looking into the horrors that reside within the subconscious then sees bright illuminous ideation when he finally looks away. And that illumination *heals* him.

As for that will wanting to "come to light on all paths, caves and ravines," I see two possible meanings, both of which can add to our understanding of the dithyramb.

On the one hand, the statement may reflect Nietzsche's desire to see the will to power within all movements that play out within the inner world, as the "blood" within the inner human being, as the engine of life. But it also reflects the theory of the Apollonian-Dionysian duality, by which every step forward into the subconscious (with its concurrent incorporation of titanic and disconsonant emotion) *rebounds* (in a musical way) with an ascension into the "heights" of Apollonian ideation and mythical being, just like music. In other words, as the actor learns to acknowledge his true feelings, he begins to discover his true Self as well. And that phenomenon of discovery, incorporation, and growth is also reflected in the dithyramb entitled "Of the Three Metamorphoses," with the camel being the assumption of the heavy subconscious, the lion being the rebound or the springboard, that inheres in all suffering, and the child being the ascension unto the supra-Self, the newly re-discovered Self, which itself represents a new beginning and certainly a new hope and direction to go even further, always further and never stopping.

> Only a very pure and free power could show this will a way into the good and

Chapter 2

> helpful; connected with a narrow mind, such a will could have been fatal to its unrestrained tyrannical desires; and in any case, a way into the open soon had to be found and bright air and sunshine had to be added.

The above statement immediately follows the previously cited statement so that it is a continuation. And Nietzsche elaborates with it on what he meant in the previous statement.

And about the will to power, one tentacle of which is the will to plumb the deepest parts of the subconscious, he says that only a special power could show the determination to plumb the subconscious in a way that would prove good and useful, but that it was very possible that the will would never find its way into goodness. And then he says that "a way into the open soon had to be found" so that "bright air and sunshine" could be added to its fate.

This goes directly to the points that, one, the will celebrates its freedom in the Apollonian realm of ideas and myths, and, two, that the illusoriness and visionariness of ideas and mythical being provide a redemptive naïveté to suffering. And this redemptory quality is most evident when the actor encounters his demons and finds them too unbearable to gaze upon until he sees his deeper Self in them, at which point they then miraculously become both bearable and incorporable — as a direct effect of the naiveté that the Apollonian Self imparts.

Dithyrambic Drama Applies to Everyone Universally

Thus, it is quite possible that, in the above first statement about the will wanting to "to come to light on all paths, caves and ravines," he is referencing the theory of the Apollonian-Dionysian duality whereby emotions within the subconscious come into consciousness. But it is also possible he is saying he wants to see the will to power in all the places within the human soul and in all the movements within the human will, which goes back to the idea that he is looking for one thing to which all of life's various movements can be attributed. And the reason it is important for us to consider that possibility is because that is precisely what the dithyrambs in his drama provide: a viewpoint of the will to power in all situations that the will to power might and does encounter along its journey. In such a way, it is possible that the statements above, particularly the first one, reflect Nietzsche's determination to see the will to power as the single engine that drives the process of life within human being.

"Thus Spoke Zarathustra" Means "Thus Spoke the Will to Power"

Insofar as Nietzsche succeeded in this delineation and then mapped its growth in *Thus Spoke Zarathustra*, at the end of each dithyramb, where he wrote "Thus spoke Zarathustra," that statement should also be understood as "Thus spoke the will to power." In other words, every great passion wants dominion over the other passions and, to the extent that it succeeds, it presents as an interpreter of all things, as we see with the sexual drive that begins to provide the criteria for all choices, thereby leading the

CHAPTER 2

subject astray sometimes. As the will to power begins its ascent unto dominion, as it most certainly does in the course of acting out Nietzsche's dithyrambic tragedy, it, too, presents itself as the interpreter of all things, and that very specific viewpoint is offered *as the focal point to begin the work of embodiment* in each of the dithyrambs comprising the drama, where each dithyramb depicts one of the many dilemmas encountered in the path of its journey toward dominion. The dithyramb says to the actor, "here is how to move forward toward dominion." Everything that is said in each of the aphorisms comprising each dithyramb says something about that movement forward, about helping the will to power achieve dominion over all the passions and beliefs — in thought and in instinct.

> The figures that an artist creates are not himself, but the order of the figures, to which he is obviously attached with the most intimate love, says something about the artist himself.

And,

> [Of Wagner's characters in his operas,] a connecting subterranean stream of moral refinement and enlargement runs through all of them, flooding them with ever more pure and purified forms - and here we stand, albeit with shameful reserve, before an innermost becoming in Wagner's own soul.

Out of Chaos, A "Musical" Will Emerges

This is precisely what can be said of Nietzsche's dithyrambs. He did not create the dilemmas between conscience and passion that are depicted in his dithyrambs. They are the stuff of life that appear invariably in everyone. But the course of their development accurately reflects Nietzsche's grappling with them and his success in overcoming them. A stream of development runs through them, a *melos*, which singularly defines their "musical" nature. In other words, one dilemma (and its overcoming) necessarily leads into the next, where an entire series of events unfold within a linear but ascending course of development, with each dilemma constituting a necessary note just like the notes in a melody. And anyone who undertakes an embodiment of his dithyrambs so that he becomes driven by the will that emerges from those dithyrambs proceeds precisely through the same development. The dithyrambist knows what lies ahead, and he writes of it in such a way as to invoke it within you. That is an entirely new experience in reading and in art.

The Dithyramb as a Universally Applicable Personal Testimonial

While there are many reasons that Nietzsche called his dithyrambic compositions "music" or "dramatic music," by which he meant music that must be acted out, as I have discussed extensively in *The Birth of Dionysia*, it is this required course of development, I believe, that lends the most plausibility to his appellation. It is the *melos* in the development that makes it dithyrambic music, which otherwise means a contiguous series of

CHAPTER 2

embodiable movements of the will whose roots in actuality render it meaningful. And make no mistake that Nietzsche had already acted out the music when he composed it afterward. Everything you find in *Thus Spoke Zarathustra* is unabridged actuality, which, by the way, runs much, much deeper than reality. That is what he references when he writes of "an innermost becoming in Wagner's [Nietzsche's] own soul."

> ... here [music] reaches up to such a height and holiness of mood that we must think of the glow of the ice and snow peaks in the Alps: so pure, lonely, difficult to reach, driftless, surrounded by the glow of love, nature rises here; clouds and thunderstorms, even the sublime are beneath it.
>
> Looking back on Tannhäuser and Holländer from [the heights mentioned above], we feel how man became Wagner: how he began dark and restless, how he stormily sought satisfaction, sought power, intoxicating pleasure, often fled back with disgust, how he wanted to throw off the burden, to forget, to deny, to renounce - the whole stream plunged sometimes into this, sometimes into that valley and bored into the darkest gorges: - on the night of this half-subterranean burrow, a star appeared

> high above him, with a sad luster, he called it as he recognized it: *Loyalty, selfless loyalty*. Why did it shine brighter and purer than everything? what secret does the word faithfulness contain for his whole being?

The Dithyramb and Self

It is the will to power within Nietzsche that began "dark and restless" within the dark and unseen subconscious, how it sought power therein and was often pushed back by the disgust that lingers within the most unaesthetic horror within, how it plumbed one deep chasm after another, when, suddenly, through mythopoeia, there appeared the shining light of Self high above. (The "star" that he references above is the same "Great star" that Zarathustra addresses at the outset of "Zarathustra's Prologue.") And what is the most beneficial thing that can be derived from the appearance of Self? It is love of Self, fidelity and loyalty to Self. And there are numerous dithyrambs that teach love of Self, like the dithyramb "Of Passing By," which teaches that, if there is no love in what you see and do, then there is no Self in it, and you should move on. And there is the dithyramb "Of the Spirit of Gravity," which teaches that love of Self will prevent the fall from the heights of spirit that are attained through an apprehension of Self back again into the lowly chaos of thought and passion.

> For in everything he thought and poetized, he expressed the image and problem of faithfulness; it is in his

CHAPTER 2

> works an almost complete set of all possible kinds of faithfulness ....

In all of the dithyrambs, the most common theme is love and obedience to Self throughout all the wanderings within the subconscious through which the will to power drives the actor. Representation of love and obedience to Self is replete throughout the drama both in explicit and subtle ways.

> It is Wagner's own primal experience, which he experiences in himself and reveres like a religious mystery: This he expresses with the word "faithfulness", this he never tires of expressing in a hundred different ways, and in the fullness of his gratitude to give the most glorious gift he has and can - that wonderful experience and realization that one sphere of his being remained faithful to the other, remained faithful out of free selfless love, the creative, innocent, lighter sphere of the dark, unrestrained and tyrannical.

It is Nietzsche who "revered like a religious mystery" the interplay between the "creative, innocent, lighter sphere" of Self and the "dark, unrestrained and tyrannical" sphere of subliminal passion, or the subconscious. And that interplay arises singularly out of love of Self. Love of Self, desire for the apprehension of Self, is the guiding principle in all of the dilemmas through which the actor passes in Nietzsche's dithyrambic drama.

Chapter 3

> In the behaviour of the two deepest forces towards each other, in the devotion of one to the other, lay the great necessity by which he alone could remain whole and himself: at the same time the only thing he did not have in his power, what he had to observe and accept, while he saw the seduction to infidelity and its terrible dangers for himself approaching again and again.

The Dithyramb and Mysticism

The interplay between the subsumption of emotion and the triggering of the mythopoeic instinct, which is the whole of "the behavior of the two deepest forces towards each other" that is mentioned above, lies outside the reach of the will. Although subsumption of subliminal sensations into consciousness does indeed require willfulness, the time it takes for the subsumption to trigger mythopoeia and the actual act of mythopoeia itself, the apprehension of the supra-Self, are totally outside the realm of will and instead are moved by forces that never enter consciousness and, thus, constitute the mysticism in the dithyrambic drama. It is for this reason that Zarathustra speaks so often about both learning to wait for himself and turning his back on himself to remove willfulness from the equation, from the mystical interplay afoot within him.

Self, Supra-Self, and Over-Self

As for the temptation to be driven by titanic emotion away from love of Self, a good example of this is Zarathustra's "last temptation" to seek out the "cry of distress," the penultimate pleading of the deepest suffering Self once it comes to the surface, in the face of the aborning over-Self, which constitutes the final and absolute transcendence of the principium individuationis, Nietzsche's Übermensch.

But there is another temptation that might lead the actor astray, and that is the seduction into beguilement with the beauty of Self. And it is a problem because Self is not the aim of life; the aim of life is the supra-Self, always the next Self, never the existing Self. And in the long run, the aim of life is beyond even the deepest Self and into the over-Self, where the will achieves its greatest freedom, a freedom beyond the limits of individuation, which is genius.

To speak of fidelity in such circumstances is to speak of love for the supra-Self, but to settle for love of an existing Self is to speak of seduction to infidelity. Thus, even in success, infidelity presents itself as a danger — even in success.

What he is writing about here are the numerous problems that the dithyrambic actor will encounter during the course of his undertaking an enactment of the drama. And he goes on to speak of other problems.

> Every one of his drives was striving for the immeasurable, every one of his joyful talents wanted to break free one by one and satisfy itself; the greater their abundance, the greater the turmoil, the more hostile their crossbreeding.

Self as Mediator to the Apollonian-Dionysian duality

Within the full spectrum of "drives," there is a duality of Apollonian and Dionysian drives, with one being all the ideational drives and the attraction to visionariness that they provide, and the other being all the emotional drives and the attraction to physical urges and impulses that they provide, respectively. And between the two, as mediator, is Self, which brings all the drives within both realms into a co-existence. But there is a very strong propensity within each realm of the drives to go their own way. And it is the mediated co-existence under the dominion of Self that is the best situation, but that goal .is not easily achieved.

> Chance and life, power, splendour, the fieriest desire to win, and even more often the merciless need to live at all tormented: everywhere were fetters and pitfalls. How is it possible

CHAPTER 3

> to remain faithful to this, to remain whole?

The Practice of Dithyrambic Drama Requires Leisure

The dithyrambic actor must also contend with the practicalities of life, which include ambitions for an esteemed place in life and perhaps wealth but, at the very least, the need to make a living. How is the actor going to pursue and achieve a completion of the life-long undertaking of Nietzsche's drama while contending with, one, the difficult pursuit of Self amidst the swirl of passions within him and, two, the demands of quotidian life? This is an important question, with which I have personally grappled many, many times, and it requires an answer. And the only answer I ever found was that the actor requires the luxury of time; he must be helped with the provision of time if his undertaking is to proceed in a timelier manner and may not necessarily require a lifetime to complete, as it did with me.

> ... how he succeeds in part and always fails in the whole, how disgust approaches him and he wants to flee, how he does not find the place where he could flee, and how he must always return to the gypsies and outcasts of our culture as one of their own.

In the above passage, he appears to be writing about Wagner's travail as an artist through life. But I see something very different and uncannily analogous to one of his dithyrambs, and I ask the reader to consider the possibility that the truer meaning of this essay is something other than what it appears to be,

It is the dithyrambic actor who only partially succeeds in his efforts to see and grasp his Self, insofar as he may succeed in bringing a demon into the light but fails to keep it in the light, or he may succeed in "seeing" his truest and deepest Self but fails as well to keep his vision in sight with even an occasional regularity.

Tragedy Invokes Nausea with Life

And after all his valiant striving, after all his numerous failures and partial victories, he inevitably falls back down from whence he came, into the chaos of fragmented thought and indulgent passion that inheres in subindividuated being, back "to the gypsies and outcasts." (See the dithyrambs "Of the Rabble" and "Of the Vision and the Riddle:" 'O Zarathustra, you stone of wisdom, you projectile, you star-destroyer! You have thrown yourself thus high, but every stone that is thrown – must fall!'") And it is the actor who struggles to uncover his Self amidst the demons that reside within his subconscious — who, while seeking refuge and repair in that brief apprehension of glorious Self, is instead overwhelmed by the nausea with life that arises from the horror of his demons. I say nausea in the sense that the will is never invigorated by the horror it encounters within the subconscious; invigoration comes later. At the first sight of demonic suffering, the will loses all vigor and, in that sense, becomes nauseous. (See the dithyramb "Of the Preachers of Death:" ""It is laborious to give birth, - say others - why give birth? One only gives birth to the

Chapter 3
miserable!")

Nietzsche's Music is the Subject of *Richard Wagner in Bayreuth*

It would be very easy to simply "read off" the above citation in a literal and conceptual way, just as we did with *Thus Spoke Zarathustra* for more than a hundred years. But it was a mistake to do that. And it would be a mistake to "read off" "Richard Wagner in Bayreuth" and not just because Nietzsche states explicitly (in "Ecce Homo") that it is not about Richard Wagner and Wagner's music but rather about himself and his *Thus Spoke Zarathustra* or, more specifically, dithyrambic music. What is to be seen beyond the surface of Nietzsche's writing in this essay is a second representation of everything we find in *Thus Spoke Zarathustra*, in all the dithyrambs, in the movements of the will. What we find in this essay is the crystalized yet un-composed, aborning image of *Thus Spoke Zarathustra*. All the permutations of the will to power, as they become evident only in its development, its ascension, all the dilemmas of passion and conscience through which the will must evolve, are already known to Nietzsche at the time he composed this essay, which was only six years before he wrote *Thus Spoke Zarathustra*, and their articulation in this reiteration should help to advance a better understanding of 'Zarathustra. More importantly, for the reader of *Thus Spoke Zarathustra* who has not yet become actor, who has not yet rendered the metaphors and begun the work of embodiment, a reading of this reiteration should provide the young actor a "jump" on that all-important work of rendition and embodiment, hopefully.

> There is a heavy air in the greater half of his life so far; it seems that he no longer hoped in general, but only from one day to the next....

The Fundaments of Will: Desire, Hope, and Belief

The idea of learning to hope "in general" as opposed to day-to-day is one of the "movements" of the will to power that is taught in one of the dithyrambs, specifically the dithyramb "Of the Thousand and One Goals." The idea of striving toward one goal after another is superseded by the value of striving for a goal which is itself the goal of many goals. In other words, the actor must strive to learn the value of over-Self beyond the value of supra-Self. There is a reason, a meaning, in the struggle to uncover the deeper Self in a continual manner, never settling for one but always digging for a deeper Self. And that meaning is to raise the deepest Self so that the deepest depths of the subconscious are raised into consciousness *permanently*, not in a transitory manner, as will often be the case for the actor. And that success with that permanence is depicted in the dithyramb "Of the Ugliest Man." Once the subconscious has been definitively raised up and kept up, then begins the work of finding the springboard that inheres in suffering, the lion that is depicted in the dithyramb "Of the Three Metamorphoses," mounting that springboard and ascending into supra-individuation and the supra-conscious, which arise on the transcendence of the principium individuationis. That ascension above the principium individuationis, where Schopenhauer's

Chapter 3

reliance on his trusty boat is raised aloft — no longer to rest upon the sea, but to rise above it — *that* is the over-Self.

As I explained in *The Birth of Dionysia*, that which Nietzsche meant by the word "Übermensch" is more than just the supra-Self; it is also the over-Self. And the over-Self is the ultimate goal of the entire drama. The over-Self is the goal, the meaning, of the numerous struggles toward the numerous gradations of being through which the actor evolves. In this, there is something much more than a quotidian hope.

Will is fundamentally comprised of desire. And hope can sustain desire, thereby imparting endurance to will. But beyond desire and hope, belief also plays a critical role within the will because belief sustains hope. It is one thing to have hope; it is quite another to have belief because belief does not develop except after many more strenuous, continual and failed efforts. Hope can be summoned, but belief must be built. And it is belief that distinguishes higher hope.

These three elements of the will, desire, hope, and belief, contribute to its endurance, and endurance is critical to will. There are individuals who are so well-endowed with endurance that their will is neither perceptible nor comprehensible to those who may be looking on, simply because their endurance is so protracted. Thus, endurance, and especially the recurrent resurrection of an extinguished hope, are traits of genius, by which I mean supra-individual ambition. And the development of sustained and far-reaching hope is critical to the will to power.

NIETZSCHE ON DITHYRAMBIC MUSIC

> As a wanderer goes through the night, with a heavy burden and deeply tired, yet excited, so it may often have been for him; a sudden death then appeared before his eyes, not as a horror, but as a tantalizing, charming ghost. Burden, road and night, all disappeared at once! - it sounded seductive.

I think it would help to make two points about the above citation. In the whole, he is writing about the actor's struggle toward his Self or supra-Self, which was Nietzsche's personal drama, beginning, as I have said, at least when he was nineteen, as evidenced by his essay "On Moods," when he writes about plumbing his moods and finding deeper moods within them, and which he then presented to the world as an embodiable and livable journey for others to undertake via his *Thus Spoke Zarathustra*.

But separately, in the first instance he references "a wanderer goes through the night." And in the second instance, he writes about a sudden death that comes to that wanderer as a relief, not as a horror. In both instances, he is writing about the same thing: the actor making his way along the journey in search of his Self while still in the absence of Self (the night). But in the first instance, he writes in metaphor, and in the second instance, less so but still not literally. When he references death, he means the death of the existing Self (proto-tragedy) that gives way to the aborning Self, thus it comes as a relief.

Chapter 3
Metaphor Made Articulation Easy for Nietzsche

Nietzsche writes in metaphor a good part of the time. And he never gives an indication that he has switched from literal writing into metaphor, which is something that particularly makes his writing difficult to understand. As I have said before, he is like the poet that reaches a particular point in his mind wherein he is speaking normally, as most people will in a conversation, and then, without warning, bursts into rhyme, or like the singer who reaches a certain frenzy in conversation and bursts into song. But the reason Nietzsche bursts out into metaphor is not because he reaches an excited frenzy but because he is writing about something that is difficult to articulate and which he finds much easier to communicate in metaphor. When he does this, it is as if he has reached up to a whole new level of communication through which his meaning flows much more easily for him than if he was forced to communicate it conventionally, which is conceptually, and which he finds very stilted and prone to stumbling. For Nietzsche, metaphor comes out much more easily and, though vague to the conventional and conceptual reader, much more precisely for anyone who is capable of rising up and listening at the same high level of metaphor in language.

"Noontide" as a Metaphor

And, in the instance of the above citation, what does he say? Again, speaking of the dithyrambic actor, he compares him to a wanderer, insofar as the actor is always looking for his Self in this emotion and that, here and there, where some emotions are superfluous or wayward and possess no remnant of Self, and others that are true and original discharges from the belly of being that resonate with Self. And to speak of such a "wanderer" searching in the "night," as opposed to the daytime, serves to add to his meaning of "wanderer" as someone searching in the absence of Self, with daytime indicating a close proximity with Self. Indeed, someone who finally has a vision of true Self, at the precise moment of Self-discovery has an experience that Nietzsche poeticized in metaphor as "the noontide," when the sun is at its highest point.

In the second half of the above citation, he speaks of the "wanderer" encountering a "sudden death." But this "death" comes as a cure, not a "horror." And this is precisely what happens to the actor who has spent a considerable amount of time looking for his Self and suddenly finds it in much deeper feelings. It is at that moment of Self-discovery, which Nietzsche calls the "noontide," that the old Self crumbles into the deeper depth that the actor has opened up within himself. This crumbling into a newly-perceived deeper depth constitutes the phenomenon we now call proto-tragedy. And it is redemptive because the burden of carrying the weight of subliminal emotion outside the purview of Self also falls away with the old Self as the incorporated subconscious becomes a dimension of the new, deeper Self. Every attribution of subconscious suffering renders that suffering comprehensible *and livable*, significantly less unbearable, as a dimension of the newer, deeper Self — and the burden falls away.

A Process of Inner Growth that is Never-ending and Leads to a Grand Hope

In the above citation, Nietzsche also writes that the

CHAPTER 3

"road" and the "night" also disappear with the arrival of a "sudden death." The "road" is the travail unto one's Self. With the discovery of the deeper Self, that "road" is gone, as is the "night," insofar as the actor is illumined within by the discovery of Self. But thereupon begins the journey unto the next deeper Self, the supra-Self, and the entire journey begins anew. And it is for this reason that Zarathustra says that the creator (the actor in the production of myth via mythopoeia) must also be a destroyer. It is for this reason that Zarathustra says "Whatever I create and however much I love it – soon I have to oppose it and my love: thus will my will have it" in the dithyramb "Of Self-Overcoming." It is also why he says "And life itself told me this secret: 'Behold,' it said, 'I am that *which must overcome itself again and again*'" in the same dithyramb.

Let there be no doubt that Friedrich Nietzsche is the most difficult writer you will ever attempt to read, but his writing is rich with meaning, and the fundamental questions he writes about, the meaning of life and especially its process, are things about which few men have written, and before Nietzsche, *no one* had ever answered.

Continuing with the very next sentence of Nietzsche's writing in this essay, he says,

> A hundred times he threw himself back into life with that short-winded hope and left all the ghosts behind him.

He is speaking of the actor resuming his journey toward Self when he says "a hundred times he threw himself back into life." Notice three things here. One, the journey requires unending and continual effort, and not just because the actor is pursuing his supra-Self, which requires numerous proto-tragic events, but also because the ultimate, supreme goal toward which he is actually striving is the over-Self, which requires a permanent resurrection of the subconscious and all the demons therein, and that is a monumental effort. And two, a short-winded hope, one that lacks the sustenance of belief, will, at the outset of the journey and for a long time into it, be his only motivation. And that is insufficient for the duration of the journey. What is needed is a firm belief in the over-Self. It is only that belief that will sustain the journey for the duration of time that will be needed to complete it. And third, notice that he defines life itself as a process of growth that proceeds upon this journey: "A hundred times he threw himself back into life." He has redefined life, or more precisely, finally defined it because no other philosopher has ever articulated the process of life, let alone its meaning. No other philosopher has ever delineated a primary engine or motivation, as Nietzsche has done with the will to power, with power being the empowerment that Self imparts to its beholder, but more importantly, the empowerment that the over-Self imparts to the will in the freedom it provides the will *beyond the limits of individuation* — in supra-individuation.

> But in the way he did it [jumped back into life with a short-winded hope], there was almost always an excess, the sign that he did not believe deeply

CHAPTER 3

> and firmly in that hope, but was only intoxicated by it.

Will as Cultivation, not Frenzy

By "intoxicated," he means it in the same way that someone who is in battle and has become downtrodden or just weary will then summon morale so as to invigorate himself to resume battle and struggle to move forward. The key word is "invigorate." Invigoration is fleeting, transitory, and momentary. And while there are fleeting and invigorating elements of the sensate realm that are useful to the will, the will is a cultivated confluence of those same emotive elements with a far-reaching vision. And hope that is used, like morale, in the moment is not as cultivated as a vision of growth that reminds its subject and then, in turn, summons hope as its counterpart. (That is a good example of the highly refined and ethereal Apollonian realm effecting its power of creativity upon the brutal and unrefined Dionysian realm.) Cultivated hope, as opposed to momentary hope, is imbued with meaning. As such, the whole process of growth of which the vision, the will, and the hope and desire are parts — itself becomes meaningful. *The presence of meaning in growth bespeaks the presence as well of a melos.* And it is this meaning, this melos, in the will to power that singularly characterizes it as music. It is because of this melos that Nietzsche calls his composition dramatic music. And dithyrambic music requires that it be embodied and acted out so that the actor becomes driven by it. It is important for the actor to cultivate meaningful hope, hope that springs from will, not hope that shimmers only in a mere moment, and that cultivation requires the development of belief.

To be more specific, the actor will make his way through many supra-Selves. One after another, he will grow deeper, more pensive, more percipient, while at the same time attaining to greater heights of spirit and visionariness, so that he becomes more insightful, more resourceful, more Self-governing. Eventually, he will reach a depth and a height wherein he is certain he will have reached the end of the line, especially after that state of mind, which is referenced as the ugliest man, has been redeemed. (See the dithyramb "The Ass Festival:" where Zarathustra speaks to the ugliest man and says, "'You seem changed, your eyes are glowing, the mantle of the sublime covers your ugliness: *what* did you do? 'Is it true what they say, that you have awakened him again [the old God who was previously proclaimed dead]? And why? Was he not with reason killed and done away with?'"

In this state, the actor will rightly think that he has been completely redeemed, completely saved, and completely reborn. And what more is there to achieve? The over-Self is what is left to achieve. And if the actor has finally and long ago realized that this is the goal of life, so that this exceptional hope has become inbred with his instincts, and if he has come to believe it firmly and resolutely, hope will come to him in that moment of dubious wonder *and will lift him up* effortlessly and inexorably toward his goal of achieving the over-Self, not as an invigorating stimulant that comes to him in the moment but as his nature. This is the difference between hope that exists by itself and hope that becomes a part of the will. The hope that the actor must build is not hope that he can summon for a shortsighted goal but rather

Chapter 3

hope that is part of a willfulness, a continuum, a melos.

> No one will ever again deny him the fame of having set the highest example for all the art of great performance.

The Dithyrambic Actor Becomes Himself a Work of Art

It is dithyrambic drama that may claim rights to being "the highest example" of great art. But that is something you can only realize after experiencing it. And unfortunately, so far, no one has had an experience with it. That should change with the publication of my essays and more and more people should begin to understand what is presented with dithyrambic drama. Insofar as the dithyramb is an embodiable representation of the will to power, which is the primary motivation of all life, profound transformations will play out within the actor who undertakes a proper rendition and enactment. I know of no other art form through which the individual is both subject and object and, in the end, himself becomes a work of art. That is a distinction to which only dithyrambic drama may lay claim.

> The innovator of simple drama, the discoverer of the position of the arts in true human society, the poetic explicator of past life observations, the philosopher, the historian, the aesthetician and critic Wagner, the master of language, the mythologist and mythopoet, who for the first time

> closed a ring around the magnificent ancient monstrous structure and dug the runes of his spirit into it - what a wealth of knowledge he had to bring together and encompass in order to become all this!

The Dithyramb is Encrypted

Regarding the innovation of simple drama, Nietzsche has taken the spectator and put him into the drama. Dithyrambic drama is not something the spectator watches unfold as we do with every other drama we know today. This is a drama that *requires* the spectator's participation so that he literally becomes the drama's actor. Without that participation, insofar as the text is encrypted in gesticulative metaphor and those metaphors point to passions and dilemmas of passion and conscience that are part of human nature, not made up, and which arise within human nature only within the development of the will to power, it is not possible to understand the encrypted text without experiencing the passions and dilemmas that the various dithyrambs depict. And the only way to experience those passions and dilemmas is to have reached a certain measure of development within the will to power. Representation of passion in writing and participation in the drama via embodiment and enactment of the depicted will is the innovation that Nietzsche achieved with dithyrambic drama.

Art as a Gateway to Culture

Regarding the discovery of the true position of the

CHAPTER 3

arts within society, it might be more accurate to speak of the discovery of the true position of the arts within a culture, not society. By culture, as opposed to society, we mean a way of thinking that has become inbred within a people. Insofar as dithyrambic drama draws the spectator into itself and transforms him into an actor, the actor undergoes changes. And one of the specific changes he undergoes is a new way of thinking. Specifically, he instinctively learns a way of thinking that is closely aligned with nature itself and leads to the discovery of the deepest and truest Self as well as transcendence of the demons with which the Self is afflicted. That is the mode of thought that Nietzsche teaches with his dithyrambs. And a way of thinking that heals man is my definition of culture. Thus, insofar as dithyrambic drama teaches this way of thinking, it stands as a gateway into the new Dionysian culture that Nietzsche has founded, which places art at the very estimable forefront of man's first truly healing culture. Dionysian culture is founded on nature, music, and art. There is nothing contrived or phony about it.

Regarding "the poetic explicator of past life observations," if we accept the proposition that the ancient Greeks discovered the inordinate value of proto-tragedy and then enshrined it in an art form which they called tragedy, then we may also accept the proposition that Nietzsche has reclaimed this art form from antiquity.

It is also worth noting, regarding the characterization "the philosopher, the historian, the aesthetician," that clearly the philosopher is Nietzsche, not Wagner, and insofar as he reclaimed from antiquity a brilliant art form for which we will be grateful for many generations to come, then we might rightly consider him to be an historian. But how is he an aesthetician?

By aesthetics, I understand the study of beauty and good taste. Good taste, especially as an element of the will to power, necessitates selection of one thing over another. And what is the criteria for selection within the will to power? Clearly, it is power or empowerment. Insofar as the apprehension of Self is simply and demonstrably empowering, there should be no question that good taste is replete throughout the development and evolution of the will to power as it is charted in his dithyrambs. As for beauty, remember that the reader of *Thus Spoke Zarathustra* becomes its actor, and, in the end, as actor, himself becomes a work of art. And one of the accomplishments that empowerment via Self achieves is profound sophrosyne. And sophrosyne exudes beauty. This is something of which you will become most convinced through your own experience, and I assure you that, upon completing the full length of the drama, inner beauty of the soul is something you will most certainly attest to.

The Dithyrambist as Myth Maker and Poet

Lastly, he refers to Wagner, though he is referring to himself indirectly, as "mythologist and mythopoet." I have identified two kinds of myth: mythical being, which is Self, and gateway myth, which is over-Self or supra-individuation. But the idea of an eternally recurring world is also a gateway myth. In both instances, that of over-Self and that of the idea of an eternally recurring world, there is no "being" entailed, which is why I identify it as a different kind of myth. And the reason I

CHAPTER 3

use the word "gateway" to describe this second kind of myth is because it is a myth that leads to the most unfettering of the will. In other words, a gateway myth refers to a place within us in which the will finds its most freedom, which also renders it the most joyful experience, far more joyful even than the discovery of the deepest and truest Self.

However, with regard to art and its creation, the most notable production of art in Nietzsche's dithyrambic tragedy is mythopoeia, the production of myth. The entire drama turns on the production of myth. In this sense, insofar as Nietzsche uses his new art form to create myth within its participating actor, then Nietzsche is a mythologist. But he is also a mythologist in his ability to lead the actor into those inner circumstances of hope and desire out of which the gateway myths arise, and to speak of the mythopoet is to speak of the sometimes-breathtaking poignancy of the text with which his dithyrambs are written. For instance, in the dithyramb "Before Sunrise," he writes "Oh heaven above me, you pure one! Deeper! You abyss of light! Looking at you, I shudder with divine desires."

Since you, the reader, probably do not yet know how to read a dithyramb, though it is my heartfelt wish that you will learn, it is unlikely you would be able to truly appreciate the poetry in the above excerpt, so I must elaborate sufficiently to bring you a little closer to it.

Myth Empowers the Will

In the first place, there is nothing abstract about this text nor anything conceptual. It represents an *echo* or reverberation of a proclamation from deep within the belly of being, your belly of being, that emerges upon the discovery of the gateway myth that is called the over-Self, when all the fetters that might possibly bind or oppress the will have been undone, causing the heart to soar to previously unknown heights. Notice that he refers to an "abyss of light." That is something which you may never have experienced outside of this drama. You surely know the "abyss of darkness," when, upon approaching within your mind and then crossing over the precipice that defines the most frightful thing you have ever experienced, you then lose your mind and your Self as a result of that transgression. But can you for just one moment take your mind into an exploration and imagine an abyss also beyond the mind wherein, instead of finding yourself about to be swallowed up by darkness and madness, you find yourself about to be redemptively bathed in an unfathomable lightness of being. Probably, you cannot. But that is precisely what the dithyrambic actor experiences upon finding the springboard that inheres in suffering, and, in this instance, the most tensile springboard that inheres only within the deepest and darkest suffering, and then mounting that springboard, and riding it the full length of its discharge. *This is a very uncommon experience*, and one that is very difficult to achieve as well. And this is what the dithyrambist Nietzsche writes about, adding, in his own words, "Now let us imagine an extreme case: that a book speaks of nothing but events which lie outside the possibility of general or even of rare experience...."

The Poignancy of Dithyrambic Poetry

Upon the reader then achieving the heights of will that are depicted in Nietzsche's dithyrambs, to have

CHAPTER 3

someone comment on it and share and help you to articulate the joy you feel in the moment *with words that are spot-on*, to my mind, constitutes some of the most beautiful poetry that man has ever written, not so much for its rhyming ability but for its poignancy. In fact, this kind of dithyrambic poetry that accompanies mythopoeia is really something more than mere poetry, which we will call dithyrambic music.

> On the whole, however, it is a dangerous sign when the spiritual struggle of a people is primarily directed towards the past, a sign of slackness, of backwardness and weakness....

Dead Myth as a Desperate Lifeline

Nietzsche has written about the phenomenon of a people in whom myth is disintegrating then reaching back in time through history for a recentering of their center of gravity to a time within that history when the myth was robust, as the fundamental Islamists are doing today in 2020 with Sharia law or as Westerners do when they speak of returning to a better time when morals were robust. In fact, such a move, reclaiming from history the fundament on which a deteriorating culture might find a leg to stand on, never works *because there is no life in that reclaimed fundament*. It was a myth that rose up in its time amongst a people who themselves bore it, created it. It is impossible to copy it or to transplant it because the life (the will, *the music*) that bore it is always absent in the transplant. The myth is only powerful when it is paired with, or itself living in, the "music" from which it emerged. It is important to ask if Nietzsche's reclamation of tragic art from antiquity is a similar, ill-fated instance. In fact, it is not. It is not a credo or a set of morals that is being reclaimed with the rebirth of tragedy, and it is not a particular myth that is being reclaimed. *What is being reclaimed is the very art form through which myth is created.* And it is an art form that we ourselves must undertake, not just believe in. One does not convert to Dionysia, as the Christians did with Christianity, upon the proclamation of a single belief. What is required to become a Dionysian is to undertake an enactment of Nietzsche's dithyrambic tragedy, therewith learning the new mode of thought that it teaches. It is both the mode of thought that reaches very deeply into one's belly of being and retrains the instincts — and the creation of a will in that process — that makes one a Dionysian, not the proclamation of a simple belief, "I believe."

Chapter 4

Dithyrambic Drama as Cultural Physician

The spirit of Hellenic culture is infinitely dispersed in our present: while the forces of all kinds are crowding in and the fruits of modern science and skill are offered as a means of exchange, the image of the Hellenic, but still very distant and ghostly, dawns again in pale features. The earth, which up to now has been sufficiently orientalized, longs again for Hellenization; whoever wishes to help it here, of course, needs speed and a winged foot to bring together the most varied and distant points of knowledge, the most remote parts of the world, in order to pass through and dominate the whole enormously stretched out field. So now a number of counter-Alexanders have become necessary, who have the most powerful power to contract and bind,

Chapter 4

> to reach the most distant threads and to prevent the fabric from being blown apart. Not to untie the Gordian knot of Greek culture, as Alexander did, so that its ends fluttered in all directions, but *to bind it after it was untied* - that is the task now. In Wagner I recognize such a counter-Alexander: he binds and ties together what was isolated, weak and casual, he has, if a medical expression is permitted, an *astringent* power: in this respect he belongs to the very great cultural powers. It rules over the arts, the religions, the different histories of peoples, and yet it is the antithesis of a polyhistory, of a spirit that only brings together and organizes: for it is a creator and animator of what has been brought together, a *simplifier of the world*.

In this chapter, Nietzsche broaches the idea that elements of ancient Greek culture could be brought into our modern culture, which goes to the point I argued in *The Birth of Dionysia* that one of his most encompassing visions was the founding of a new culture, with his dithyrambic tragedy being the gateway for initiates into that culture.

He goes on to say that modern culture has been "sufficiently orientalized" up to now, by which I presume he means that the instinctual reaction to tragedy has become trained on resignation, instead of invigoration, which is the Dionysian reaction. And he says that, in light of that satiety, the pendulum is now swinging in the opposite direction, back toward whence it began its swing, which would be within the Hellenic culture, which is distinguishable from Alexandrian culture, with that culture being more of a state-forming (Apollonian) mindset than the Hellenic (Dionysian) art-healing mindset.

In that reformation, if that is what we may call it, what is needed is to find and bring together all the existing fragments of Hellenism that we may find scattered amongst ourselves and then animate those parts so that they attain life and then, most importantly, to create anew with those living parts. The key phrase here is "create anew" because it will do no good to take what the ancient Greeks created and then plug those good things into modern culture. What is needed is to recognize what is unchangeable innate nature and what is changeable habit or changeable unnatural human nature and focus on that. And a way of thinking is changeable habit. Change the way a person thinks and perhaps they will see their own innate human nature more clearly. More importantly, if there exist within human nature phenomena whose outcome could miraculously "cure" unnatural human nature, and if a way of thinking that enabled a person to see their own nature more clearly gave that person access to the thaumaturgic phenomena, that would be an extraordinary achievement toward the salvation of humankind. And that is the role that dithyrambic drama plays within Dionysian culture.

CHAPTER 4
Dithyrambic Tragedy as Life's Most Valuable Asset

Nietzsche views himself as an Alexander-like historical figure, but in a reversed sense. Whereas Alexander conquered the furthest outposts of the world and spread the Greek way to those outposts, Nietzsche is doing the opposite by taking those far-scattered parts and reigning them back in to a containment within the mind's focus and then simplifying those parts into, in this case, the miraculous phenomenon of proto-tragedy, which he recognizes as the quintessence of ancient Greek culture, the jewel atop the ancient crown of wisdom.

> A reformation of the theater is expected of him: if he were to succeed in it, what would be done for that higher and more distant task?
>
> Well, that would change and reform modern man: so necessary is one thing hanging on another in our newer world that whoever pulls out a nail will make the building sway and fall. The same would be expected of any other real reform, as we are saying here of Wagner, with the appearance of exaggeration. It is not at all possible to produce the highest and purest effect of theatrical art without not innovating everywhere, in custom and state, in education and transport. Love and justice, which have become powerful at one point, namely here in

> the field of art, must continue to spread according to the law of their inner need and cannot return to the motionlessness of their former pupation.

Insofar as ancient Greek culture transformed its people into a progeny of geniuses who then went on to transform all the departments of life, like mathematics, astronomy, medicine, philosophy, and insofar that the ancient Greeks alone invented the art of tragedy, which we now know is an invigorator of sub-individuated human nature (madness) that transforms it into supra-individuated human nature (genius), then I would contend that Nietzsche is indeed an Alexander-like historical figure who has singlehandedly resurrected tragedy and, with it, founded a new culture, which will be called Dionysia. And we should expect those extraordinary individuals of the future who are borne out of this new culture likewise to transform all the departments of life, just as they did the last time around.

> If we are to understand how the position of our arts in relation to life is a symbol of the degeneration of this life, how our theatres are a disgrace to those who build them and visit them, we must completely retrain ourselves and be able to see the familiar and everyday as something very unusual and intricate. A strange clouding of judgment, a badly concealed addiction to pleasures, to

CHAPTER 4

> entertainment at all costs, scholarly consideration, pomposity and acting with the seriousness of art on the part of the performers, a brutal greed for financial gain on the part of the corporate world, the hollowness and thoughtlessness of a society which thinks of the people only as far as it is useful or dangerous, and attends theatres and concerts without ever being reminded of duties - all this together forms the dull and perishable air of our present state of art.

It is difficult to make this paragraph comprehensible to a reader who has yet to experience the profoundly transformative powers of dithyrambic drama. If nothing more, I would ask that the reader at least accept the proposition that a reading of *Thus Spoke Zarathustra* will lead him or her directly to their Self. No other book can make that claim, and, if you think that there are other books that can make that claim, then I have not made my point. I do not mean that the book will lead you to experience profound passion, as some books do. I mean that you will behold a vision of your Self, which you will recognize as your long-lost Self. I mean "Self" in the strict sense of the world, as myth. Upon attaining an apprehension of Self, your whole way of *experiencing* your emotions will change so that you will experience them with a new depth, clarity, and meaning. And as you advance further into this process of plumbing deeply into your emotions, yet another vision of Self will come to you. And that newer, deeper vision of Self will transform you *yet again*.

If you accept that proposition, then, in comparison, that which we call drama today pales in comparison. In my time, drama has been reduced to entertainment and some of that entertainment consists of a celebration of gruesome expressions of some of the most base and ugly emotions, like Romans at the Colosseum. With the dithyramb and specifically with dithyrambic tragedy, drama has been elevated to the position of guardian of good health and the emergence of a higher will within the human soul.

> For art is not there for the struggle itself, but for the pauses before and in the midst of it, for those minutes when, looking back and anticipating, one understands the symbolic, when, with a feeling of quiet tiredness, an invigorating dream approaches us.

Nietzsche now reveals several very important insights into his meaning and use of the word "art" that the reader should ponder fully.

A Definition of Art

The most important thing to understand about his use of the word "art" is that it is not a reference to art as we find it in literature, auditory music (which I distinguish from dramatic or dithyrambic music), sculpting, painting, or any of the physical arts. He means it in relation to the will, as a phenomenon that is meaningful to the will and specifically the will to power. As I explained quite extensively in my other books, art, as a phenomenon relating to the growth of the will, occurs as mythopoeia,

CHAPTER 4

be it the creation of mythical being, like Self, or a gateway myth, like the idea of an eternally recurring world, through which the will becomes unfettered or free of some great and enduring yoke. It is the creation of the myth that constitutes the act of art. When Nietzsche says "art," he means myth and its creation, mythopoeia.

Thus, when he says that "art is not there for the struggle itself," he means art does not play a role in the day in and day out existence of the will. Art does not muster the will, does not call it to rise to the occasion. Art does not assist in the gathering that the will carries out for itself in search of that which resists it. Instead, he says that art exists "for the pauses before and in the midst" of the struggle. And by "pauses," he means obstacles, periods of development within the will when it can go no further along the course of its development, when it gets stuck.

Art in the Will as Idea

Then he says something very insightful but very vague. He says that art rears its head and steps into the course of development "when, looking back and anticipating, one understands the symbolic." What he does not say, but should have said, is that, in its understanding of the "symbolic," which arises directly from its understanding of the past and its anticipation of the future, something happens that enables the will, delivers it from the pause, and moves it forward.

In other words, the individual, in the course of pursuing something he wants, comes upon an obstacle that keeps him just one step away from achieving his goal and getting what he wants, and he looks back on where he has been thus far and everything he has done to successfully make his way thus far, and he understands something that he previously did not understand and which comes to him as if out of nowhere. And most importantly, whatever it was that he previously did not understand and now does and which came to him as if out of nowhere, comes to him in a flash, like a flash of bright lightening, as Zarathustra would say in "The Tree on the Mountainside." It is an idea and, quite remarkably, it enables his will *to move forward.*

Love of Myth and Life

In a much more sophisticated instance, consider the lot of an individual who has been plumbing the depth of his feelings. And he repeatedly comes upon a deeply consternating subliminal emotion or mood that disturbs him but that he cannot understand and certainly *cannot allow himself to feel it.* And he looks back on where he has already been in the course of his will, of his wanting to fathom his deep feelings, and he knows that, as in the past, if he plumbs them long enough, quite suddenly he will see his Self in the feeling, as he has already done many times. And sure enough, after a very lengthy and very pensive consideration that, in a curious way, required a deliberate stepping away from the situation followed by a re-focusing, many times, and quite suddenly, he realizes his deeper Self, which is more brilliant and more gripping than the last experience with the shallower Self, in accordance with the greater depth that he was able to plumb this time around. He understands the gradations of being, and he understands most importantly that they exist. And, in that understanding and the subsequent anticipation it invokes, he sees a vision: his Self — in the future, not the present. And that vision encompasses and reveals many things about the entire realm of emotions. But it speaks symbolically and without actually articulating anything yet with the greatest clarity and certainty about that which it speaks, and all in a flash. If you can imagine that.

Most importantly, the vision of Self, albeit dream-like in appearance and effect insofar as it is an illusory creation of art, enables and invigorates the will because it provides a way forward in the effort to subsume the subconscious realm. The individual who comes upon a subliminal mood that he cannot understand and therefore is unable to incorporate into his consciousness is able to move forward once he recognizes the mood as a dimension *of his own being*. Thus, it enables the will. And while his journey toward Self has been a tiring struggle, his success invigorates him toward a continued struggle, surely.

Lastly, from the above paragraph, he says that art exists so that "the bow" does not break. Coincidentally, I used the same analogy of the bow and arrow to explain the ascension unto supra-individuation in the face of the most intense subliminal suffering, particularly fear. Art provides wings at the cliffside.

Art as the Creation of Genius

Supra-individuation results from a transcendence of the principium individuationis via the springboard that inheres in suffering. To put it another way, it is only when the actor confronts his subliminal torment by bringing it fully into consciousness that the will, which cannot move beyond the momentous obstacle presented by that torment, is stretched to its limits and forced to find a way out. And the only way out that it finds is to mount the springboard in suffering to rise up above the abyss presented by that suffering. It is always a guttural and instinctive event. And that rising up leads directly to a transcendence of the limits of Self and the creation of the supra-conscious. Beyond those limits and within the realm of the supra-conscious is the human condition we call "genius."

What is important to understand in all this is that the momentum within the springboard, which results from the tension within the bow, and the extent of the transcendence are both directly proportional to the stress that the will experiences in the confrontation and the subsequent blocking of the will's path forward. And finally, both the transcendence of the principium individuationis and the ascension into the supra-conscious, which arises directly out of the sub-conscious, do not exist outside of the tensing of the bow. Their creation is an act of art. Thus, art exists so that the bow does not break. Art saves man precisely at that moment in which his utter destruction is imminent. As such, art is a savior.

Before leaving this paragraph, I would like to point out two statements within it that bear some comment.

> Now how could one endure this triple feeling of inadequacy if in his struggles, aspirations and perishing he did not already recognize something sublime and meaningful and did not learn from tragedy to enjoy the rhythm of great passion and the sacrifice of it.

CHAPTER 4

The question he asks is how can the suffering individual endure his suffering and also struggle and hope to overcome it if he did not perceive something very special as a reward for that struggling. On the one hand, the suffering individual who thus struggles will gain the benefit of an increasing communion with emotion, which is no small thing and may only become apparent in the process. The difference without that communion is a monotone, if not boring, and thoroughly cerebral experience with one's inner nature as opposed to a more musical, more pronounced experience. On the other hand, proto-tragedy presents an anticipation of something very special in its outcome, which validates the enormous sacrifice that is entailed in its undertaking, specifically the death of the current Self for the aborning supra-Self and the incorporation of deeply distressful emotion, which is music to the ears of a sufferer.

> Art, of course, is not a teacher and educator of immediate action; the artist is never in this sense an educator and adviser....

Art as Justice in Life

One might wonder why he would say that art is not a teacher when he uses his dithyrambic drama to teach everything he learned about life. The new dithyramb is an art form, and, in the above sentence, he is not referring to an art form when he says art cannot teach. He is referring to art in and of itself, per se, a very specific and particular phenomenon, namely the creation of myth, mythopoeia. Mythopoeia is a deeply instinctual event and a loud pronouncement of new laws upon the mind. It is very powerful and very transformative.

The new dithyramb is a literary representation of the will, specifically the will to power, and it is highly instructive in the process of life insofar as life is driven by the will to power and the new dithyramb offers an embodiment of that will. As the actor becomes driven by that will, he undertakes the process of life and enters into those situations wherein the will is met with extreme opposition. And it is in those moments of extreme opposition that mythopoeia is invoked, which constitutes the art, the creativity, in the art form. But there is no offer of instruction in that creation, *just doing*. Mythopoeia does not teach and it does not show the way forward because it *is* itself the way forward. Mythopoeia says nothing about anything until it finally comes into being. And it certainly says nothing about the will's path forward. Mythopoeia delivers, and what it delivers is redemptory illusion, which has its greatest impact on the suffering out of which it sprang into being. It is in this sense that he says art does not teach. Art moves us forward but it does not show us *how* to move forward. Only the will shows how.

Life is not Possible without Tragedy

In the final paragraph of this chapter four, he writes about proto-tragedy as something very special, so special, in fact, that mankind cannot live without it. And he proclaims its re-birth in the modern era (under his tutelage) as a milestone in the course of Western culture. And he places its value and special-ness in its ability to enable the individual to consecrate himself to the super-personal, to something greater than himself, or, as I would put it, the supra-Self.

This observation becomes easily comprehensible upon experiencing proto-tragedy. In fact, it is a glorious experience for the actor who has spent a tremendous amount of time and effort to gather the parts of his Self amid the chaotic swirl of passion and thought that results from sub-individuation, who finally has before his eyes the beautiful vision of Self and all the empowerment that results from that vision, to then sense within his depths a deeper, more comprehensive, more empowering vision of Self, the supra-Self, and finally to find the wisdom and the will to allow that beautiful vision to fall asunder in order to grasp or apprehend the deeper vision. That is the value of proto-tragedy. It enables life. Life is not possible without it. Philosophically speaking, proto-tragedy enables becoming within a world that is dependent upon and, at times, totally dominated by being.

Actuality versus Reality

What we have playing out within man are two realms of phenomena: actuality, which is a realm entirely of becoming and based upon the physical (or Dionysian) world of emotion, which is also a world of music, where music speaks and one learns to listen for it, and reality, which is a realm entirely of being and based upon the illusory and fictive (or Apollonian) world of ideation (or myth). And the two disparate worlds must find a way to accommodate each other so that they may interact with each other. Proto-tragedy provides that accommodation, singularly.

Reality is essentially an interpretation of actuality, and it is an interpretation based on (i.e., viewed through the perspective of) Self, which itself is an entirely fictive, thus illusory, creation. Self is the product of art in the life process. However, with the addition of being to that interpretation, which is what happens with mythopoeia, then reality becomes a *reconstruction* of actuality. And it is that reconstruction that gives rise to the two disparate realms of actuality and reality, which is reducible to Nietzsche's notion of the Apollonian-Dionysian duality, insofar as actuality is founded on the phenomenon of emotion and reality is founded on the phenomenon of idea or myth. And the juxtaposition of reality with actuality constitutes a profound contradiction in human nature: the existence of a world of being alongside the existence of a world of becoming. But the world of being is also essential to life, just as proto-tragedy is essential. Life without an idea and a sense of being is also not possible. It is a quite necessary invention or creation. And proto-tragedy cures this primordial contradiction by accommodating being and enabling becoming.

Chapter 5

Dithyrambic Drama as a Simplification of the World

> Wagner placed present life and the past under the light of a knowledge that was strong enough to be able to see with it in unusual breadth: that is why he is a simplifier of the world; for the simplification of the world always consists in the fact that the gaze of the recognizer has once again mastered the immense fullness and desolation of an apparent chaos, and is now crowding together what was once considered incompatible. Wagner did this by finding a relationship between two things that seemed foreign and cold as if they were living in separate spheres: between *music and life* and also between *music and drama*. Not that he invented or created these relationships: they are there and actually lie at everyone's feet: just as

CHAPTER 5

> the great problem always resembles the noble rock over which thousands walk until finally someone picks it up.

He says many things here, which we can only begin to understand by sorting them out first. In the first place, he talks about a simplification of the world. In order to write a drama that depicts the course of life from beginning to end, it is necessary to already have simplified everything that plays out in that course, which means reducing it to a simpler course of action that depicts all the major events comprising that process of growth — and nothing else.

Dithyrambic Drama as the Will to Power

Next, he says that Wagner, by which he meant himself, was able to achieve these simplifications by discovering a relationship that exists between things within the inner world of man, by which he most certainly meant the Apollonian-Dionysian duality, which is the relationship between emotion (which includes the will) and idea (which includes myth and the lesser concept). And that simplification is called the will to power.

But Nietzsche characterizes the relationship he discovered as that between music and life, which he then re-characterizes more explicitly as that between music and drama. It is easy enough for us to understand what he means by life as well as what he means by drama, although there is a huge difference between modern, theatrical drama and dithyrambic drama. But what does he mean by "music?" I would argue that he does not mean auditory music which we listen to with our ears. I would suggest that he means will, which we listen for with our intuition. Thus, to rephrase what he meant, he discovered a relationship between will and drama, and we still have not clearly defined what he meant by "drama."

Dithyrambic Drama as a True Depiction of Reality

Lastly, he says that this relationship between things that are Apollonian and Dionysian, or things that are emotional and ideational, are not relationships that he conjured or imagined or in any way constructed. "They are there and actually lie at everyone's feet," which means the events that are depicted within a dithyrambic drama are real, actual, and realistic, not conjured or fictional. And, unless the reader has learned how to read a dithyramb, which includes learning how to embody the will it depicts, it might be very difficult for him or her *to believe* that a dithyramb depicts reality or, more specifically, actuality. But that is what you must grasp.

Dithyrambic Drama as Instruction via Feeling, not Concept

Next, in the following citation, he begins to speak of the problem that arises with communication between two people. And he speaks specifically of the miscommunication that results from language that denotes thought and concept, as opposed to language that denotes feeling, which is an entirely novel use of language that you, the reader, may not be able to imagine. But that is the language in which the dithyramb is composed. It is a language that denotes feeling and specifically the feelings that comprise the will.

Chapter 5

> He first became aware of a state of emergency that is as far-reaching as civilization now connects peoples: language has fallen ill everywhere, and the pressure of this monstrous disease is weighing on the whole of human development. Language has had to climb continually onto the last rungs of what it can achieve in order to grasp the realm of thought, the opposite of feeling, as far as possible from the strong emotional excitement to which it was originally able to respond in all simplicity. Man, in his need, can no longer make himself known to language, that is, he cannot truly communicate: In this darkly felt state of affairs, language has become a force in itself everywhere, which now grasps and pushes people as if with ghostly arms, where they do not really want to go....

In the above, he denotes a distinction between language that seeks to communicate thought and language that seeks to communicate feeling. He postulates that language, in its original form, was used to communicate feeling, which it did very simply. And only afterwards, it was used to communicate thought, which it must struggle to achieve.

> As soon as they try to communicate with one another and to unite in a work, the madness of general

> concepts, even of pure word sounds, seizes them, and as a result of this inability to communicate, the creations of their common sense bear the mark of not understanding themselves, inasmuch as they do not correspond to the real needs, but only to the hollowness of those words and concepts that are so violent: thus humanity adds to all its sufferings the suffering of the *Convention*, that is, of the Convention in words and actions without a convention of feeling.

This statement represents a very radical deviation from the use of language and literature in the arts that has existed as a tradition since the days of denoting grain and stock by carving symbols into clay tablets, which I think might rightly be called the beginning of time.

The Dithyrambist Creates Will with Embodiable Passions

Language, he says, has never been used to represent feelings. Language has always been used to denote things and concepts, but not feelings. The dithyramb is Nietzsche's new invention that uses language to denote feelings. And just as when a reader sees a word that references a complicated concept and requires time to formulate the concept, so, too, does Nietzsche's language, which we will call dithyrambic music, reference some passions with which the listener might be unfamiliar and requires the time to find it within himself. And using his newfound language, Nietzsche found himself capable of transmitting very specifically the exact passion he wanted to depict, so that there is a great deal of understanding between himself and his readers (or listeners) regarding exactly what he means and what he means to do with that passion. Given these facts, I do not think there has ever been a more precise or more impactful use of language as what we find in dithyrambic music.

The Birth of a New Culture via Dithyrambic Drama

He speaks of uniting in a work. That is a novel concept: to unite in a work? What he means is that he wants the reader to experience the emotions he has depicted in his dithyrambs and, in that sense, to unite with him and with the others who experience his dithyrambs and therewith become driven by a will. That kind of experience, which is the foundation of a new culture, is an emotional and willful experience and cannot be achieved via the communication of concepts.

> ... and as a result of this inability to communicate, the creations of their common sense bear the mark of not understanding themselves, inasmuch as they do not correspond to the real needs, but only to the hollowness of those words and concepts ...

Quite simply, all he is saying is that a man who wishes to communicate his simplified understanding of the common sense within us *cannot* achieve that transmission via language that deals in concepts because concept does not bespeak need but emotion does.

> ... in the decline of languages, one is the slave of words; Under this constraint no one is able to show himself, to speak naively, and few at all are able to preserve their individuality, in the struggle with an education which does not believe to prove its success by meeting clear feelings and needs in an educative way, but by weaving the individual into the web of "clear concepts" and teaching him to think correctly: as if it had any value to make someone a correctly thinking and reasoning being if it has not succeeded in making him a correctly feeling one beforehand.

He makes a good point about giving a young man or young woman a good mind, one that is also grounded in the reality of their emotions. as the fundament upon which a life will be built. And I think it is obvious that the ability to think straight is far more valuable than the ability to think correctly. Yet, everywhere we teach logic as an exercise in the correct way to think. But nowhere do we teach the best way to think intuitively. *Thus Spoke Zarathustra* is, in fact, an exercise in the best way to think intuitively. Even better, it is also an exercise in the best way to learn how to feel intuitively. And that exercise, though it may last a lifetime, ends in a solid and well-grounded mind as well.

Chapter 5

> ... this music is a return to nature, while at the same time it is the purification and transformation of nature; for in the soul of the most loving people the compulsion for that return has arisen, and *in their art nature transformed into love resounds*.

Dithyrambic Music and Love of Nature

"This music" he refers to is the music of Beethoven and Mozart and others of that age. And he calls it a return to nature. But when he refers to the "purification and transformation" that results from that music, I believe he is referring to human nature that is purified and transformed by that music. He says that the music compels within the soul of its listeners a yearning to return to nature. And in their musical compositions, the artists who composed it transformed nature itself into a resounding love. And precisely the same may be said of dithyrambic music, the literary representation of human will, insofar as it is his own inner nature that the actor celebrates throughout the drama. And it is a love of that inner human nature that Nietzsche has created with his dithyrambic tragedy.

> The relationship between music and life is not only that of one kind of language to another kind of language, it is also the relationship of the perfect auditory world to the entire visual world.

Art as Passion and Vision

He says that the relationship between music and life is a relationship between "the perfect auditory world" and the entire visual world. This goes to his theory of the Apollonian-Dionysian duality, which I argue theorizes that will arising out of the realm of emotions prompts the formulation of idea and myth, with myth being either a fictive vision of being or a gateway idea that vastly enables the will. But the entire relationship is reducible to passion and vision. Even though he specifically denotes music here in this passage as being the auditory form of music, as opposed to the dramatic form of music (i.e., the will), he will go on in this essay to make the same argument regarding this relationship as existing between will and mind (i.e., the entire Apollonian world), the argument being that a confluence of emotion as will *speaks* to the mind and *moves* it to look more deeply into the realm of emotion, wherein the mind grows beyond its limits.

The Town Called "The Pied Cow" or "The Motley Cow"

This next passage is a commentary on his use of the metaphor of the town he mentions in "Zarathustra's Prologue" as the Pied Cow, which also translates as the Motley Cow. And before we begin, let us take a look specifically at the German phrase he uses in his appellation. The phrase is "die bunte Kuh." And I would direct your focus to the word "bunte," which translates to "colorful." Hollingdale translated a "colorful cow" to a "Pied Cow," and I think that is a miss. Other translators arrived at a "Motley Cow," which I think is a better

CHAPTER 5

translation, given what I know to be the particular state of mind that is depicted in the Prologue and referred to as "the town called the Motley Cow and, thus, also which gesticulative metaphor would best point to that state of mind. But there is also an idiomatic use of the German word "bunte" that means "a riot of discordant colors," with the word "riot" emphasizing the particular meaning, and I think that would be the best translation. But what is that state of mind that Nietzsche would gesticulate as "The Cow that is a Riot of Discordant Colors?"

In this next passage (and I cite the entire, lengthy passage), Nietzsche elaborates on his understanding of the wayward state of mind that results from suffering, and he compares it to "a dress in colorful rags."

> Taken as an apparition to the eye and compared with the earlier apparitions of life, the existence of the newer people shows an unspeakable poverty and exhaustion, despite the unspeakable colourfulness through which only the most superficial glance can feel happy. One only has to look a little sharper and dissect the impression of this violently moving play of colours: isn't the whole thing like the shimmering and flashing of countless little stones and pieces borrowed from earlier cultures? Isn't everything here inadequate pomp, imitated movement, presumptuous exteriority? A dress in colourful rags for the naked and cold? An apparent

dance of joy, expected of the suffering? Miens of exuberant pride, carried to the show by a deeply wounded man? And in between, veiled and concealed only by the speed of movement and whirl - grey impotence, gnawing discord, industrious boredom, dishonest misery! The appearance of modern man has become entirely illusory; he is not himself visible in what he now presents, much rather hidden; and the rest of the inventive artistic activity which has survived among a people, such as the French and Italians, is applied to the art of this hiding. Wherever "form" is now demanded, in society and entertainment, in literary expression, in the intercourse of states with one another, it is involuntarily understood to be a pleasing appearance, the antithesis of the true concept of form as a necessary form, which has nothing to do with "pleasing" and "unpleasing", because it is necessary and not arbitrary. But even there, where among the peoples of civilization form is not expressly demanded, they do not possess the necessary form either; they are not so happy in their striving for pleasing appearance, but

CHAPTER 5

> are at least as eager. *How pleasing* appearances are here and there, and why it must please everyone that modern man should at least strive to appear, is something which everyone feels to the extent that he himself is a modern man. "Only the galley slaves know each other," says Tasso, "but we only politely *misjudge* the others, so that they should misjudge us again.

Now, in order to fully understand this, we need to deconstruct it, and keep in mind that what we most want to understand is his use of the phrase "motley cow" (or "Pied Cow") in "Zarathustra's Prologue," and, more specifically, the state of mind to which the metaphor points *as we see it within ourselves*.

> ... the existence of the newer people shows an unspeakable poverty and exhaustion, despite the unspeakable colourfulness through which only the most superficial glance can feel happy.

By "newer people," he is talking about a person who is a part of our modern Western culture. In summa, he is saying that when we present ourselves to one another, it is not our true, genuine Self we present, but rather our dressed up, glamorized Ego. And he speaks of the pretty "dress" in which we glamorize our presentable Ego as a colorful dress, glittering with "countless little stones," which are meant to distract the observer away from our true Self toward the disingenuous Ego.

He also says something very interesting. He says that, though an individual may be a deeply suffering individual, he nevertheless carries miens of exuberant pride and an appearance of joy, which is an entirely phony appearance, *to the show*. By "show," he means the moment when two individuals come together and therein spread out their tail feathers for each other for no other reason than to impress upon each other. In "Zarathustra's Prologue," he uses the phrase "marketplace," which means something similar, a moment of coming together and fanning, but actually he means something much more specific in that instance. He means when an individual comes together with his Self, the moment when an individual looks inward to face himself, his conscience. And therein, too, the individual throws up a spread of glittering stones to impress *himself*. It actually gets much more complicated in the Prologue after that initial moment of looking inward to face oneself, which is beyond the scope of what I wish to explain just now. But there are very few instances throughout Nietzsche's writing wherein he elaborates at all about his use of the metaphor "marketplace" and "Motley Cow," and this is one of them, so it is important to consider it.

Within this same paragraph, he goes on to speak of "form," and by "form" I believe he means form in the sense that he uses the same word to write about the Apollonian side of the Apollonian-Dionysian duality, when he speaks of the god Apollo as a form-giving power. In other words, with "form," he means the creation of being within a totally formless world; he means Self.

CHAPTER 5
Ego Precludes the Practice of Dithyrambic Drama; It Requires Self

> The appearance of modern man has become entirely illusory; he is not himself visible in what he now presents, much rather hidden....

And,

> Wherever "form" is now demanded, in society and entertainment, in literary expression, in the intercourse of states with one another, it is involuntarily understood to be a pleasing appearance, the antithesis of the true concept of form as a necessary form, which has nothing to do with "pleasing" and "unpleasing", because it is necessary and not arbitrary.

He says we have lost sight of what it means to be true and original, to engage our Self, with each other. And though he does not say it explicitly, he also means that we have lost sight of our ability to be "real" with ourselves, which, in fact, is a necessity of life.

Amidst all this "tail spreading" and deliberate, forgiving misjudgment about what is real and necessary about Self within modern culture (i.e., a lack of integrity with one's own conscience) now comes dithyrambic drama, which demands only the highest integrity in dealings with Self and requires a measure of honesty toward Self that can only be achieved with an equal measure of courage.

> In this world of forms and desired misjudgment, the souls filled with music now appear - for what purpose? They move according to the great free rhythm, in noble honesty, in a passion that is super-personal, they glow from the powerful, calm fire of music that gushes out of inexhaustible depth into the light - all this for what purpose?

A Definition of Dithyrambic Music

Notice also that he describes those who would be naturally inclined toward Self and away from Ego and might likely partake in his dithyrambic drama as "souls filled with music" and as glowing from the "music" that comes from an "inexhaustible depth." The question I put to the reader is what does he mean here by "music" when speaking of such individuals, most specifically himself, who possess a naturally occurring drive toward Self despite an entire world of very forceful distractions within themselves that are constantly pulling them away from Self and toward Ego. And as an answer to that question, I say, simply, that it is the flow of interactivity that exists between Self and emotion as well as idea, with emotion flowing into Self (as myth) and idea flowing out. *That is music*; the music is in that flow. Above all else, what must be understood about this flow is that it is meaningful, which is no small thing and should not be underestimated, and necessary, which means nothing about it is extraneous or superfluous. *That* is dramatic music: the

CHAPTER 5

relationship, the flow, that exists between actuality and reality, between Self and the nature that inheres in emotion, with emotion originating from deep within actuality where Nature resides.

In the next long paragraph, Nietzsche gives an excellent clue, perhaps the best I have seen anywhere, of what he means with his use of the word "music."

> He, however, who feels genuine and fruitful life in him, which at present can only be described by the one term "Music," could he allow himself to be deceived for one moment into nursing solid hopes by this something which exhausts all its energy in producing figures, forms, and styles?

"*He who feels* [emp. added] genuine and fruitful life in him" is to be "described by the one term 'Music.'" That is the most explicit definition of music he will ever give us outright, anywhere in anything he wrote.

And he compares "genuine and fruitful life" to something which might rightly be regarded as an antithesis to the musical soul. He compares it to egotistical man, the man in whom the Ego has grown enormously, so that the individual no longer acts or thinks naturally, and who engages in and misidentifies society as culture. The antithetical egotistical man is the man who does not heed his conscience.

He spent all of the preceding paragraph describing this egotistical type of man who seeks to escape himself in the company of other men and who seeks to deceive the world about himself using fancy and glittery "colors," as the Ego will do. And that is precisely his meaning of "motley" or "pied" in the first dithyramb named "Zarathustra's Prologue," in which he mentions a town called the Motley Cow. He is describing a state of mind in which egotistical man ignores his conscience and attempts to present himself as someone other than who he is, all glittered up. This egotistical mode of thought that derives from the dominion of Ego over Self is nothing more than "a game invented by the idle desire to produce [a glittery] effect [with which] to deceive others." And it is a mode of thought, a mindset, that is antithetical to the mindset that Nietzsche refers to as musical.

But is that how egotistical man presents himself to himself? Yes, it is, and he achieves it only by ignoring his conscience.

Nietzsche wrote his dithyrambs for the man of conscience, not the egotistical man. And I do not mean "man of conscience" as a trope. I mean an individual who listens to what his conscience says in regular matters as much as weighty matters. Moreover, a scientifically minded man would not do well with his dithyrambs; nor would a man who cannot muster the most severe form of integrity with regard to his conscience. The man who listens to his conscience is a musical man, as Nietzsche himself stated above, because the conscience speaks to him as if *through music*, which is to say immediately and without the aid of thought. And the conscience speaks in a language that primarily uses intuition and instinct and only secondarily thought, which means the conscience is not swayed by egotistical thought that is unnatural and wayward. The mind may be swayed by unnatural thought, but not the conscience. Emotion and a curious observance of strictly defined limits (which goes to the Self) are also

CHAPTER 5

communicated via conscience. But in any case, conscience does not use concept in its communication with us. It is only the mind that uses concept to speak to us, and the conscience is different from the mind. Thus, the conscience speaks to us musically but the mind does not. Above all, "music" does not speak through concept. And the text in which Nietzsche composed his dithyrambs is precisely this kind of music: a communication via intuition, emotion, instinct and strictly defined limits — and it is entirely devoid of concept. Concept will come into play, certainly, but only in the understanding that follows afterward in the mind, not in the initial communication with the conscience.

But how does one communicate if not with words that denote concepts, the fundaments of communication with the mind? Again, the dithyramb does not speak to your mind; it speaks to your conscience. And how do you listen to your conscience? Purely through intuition. And it is purely through intuition that the dithyramb speaks to you. The dithyrambist communicates with gesticulative metaphors instead of concepts, and the metaphors are gesticulative insofar as they point to (or denote) something arising from within the conscience, whether it is an instinct (to do the right thing, for instance), an emotion, a conflict of conscience and emotion, or a violation or redefining of the limits, the boundaries, of conscience. It is possible that one can draw a concept of what is being pointed out, but, in the end, the actor *must* reach down into himself to reach the object of the gesticulation and therewith delimit and isolate it with loving hands because it is upon that instinct or that conflict that the drama proceeds *as if within a melody* to the next object of gesticulation along the grand course whose ultimate aim is to see the vision, the vision of Self.

That said, while we have a clearer understanding of his use of the word "music" as the *intuitable* language in which the conscience speaks to the individual who heeds his conscience, as opposed to a language of concepts, as in the communicability between mind and Ego, we still need a clearer understanding of the word "music," which we will achieve shortly, at the end of this essay, in the summary.

Transformative Art Will Also Transform Society

Moving forward, Nietzsche asks those who would be moved by dithyrambic music and who would undertake and complete his dithyrambic tragedy, to what humanitarian end might they then be moved?

> Help me, he calls out to all who can hear, help me to discover that culture of which my music is the rediscovered language of correct perception, think about the fact that the soul of music now wants to form a body for itself, that it seeks its way through all of you to visibility in movement, action, institution and custom! There are people who understand this call and there are more and more of them; they understand again for the first time what it means to base the state on music, something that the older

CHAPTER 5

> Hellenes not only understood but also
> demanded of themselves....

That culture of which dithyrambic music is the rediscovered language is Dionysia, a new culture, which Nietzsche himself has founded. And if we define culture as a mode of thought, particularly one that enables suffering man to heal, if not also redeem, his suffering, then, indeed, dithyrambic drama is the foundation of a new culture insofar as it teaches an entirely new way of thinking that is closely aligned with the dictates of conscience and that most certainly leads to the healing of suffering man and the redemption of that suffering in a very meaningful way.

And surely, those who complete his drama, thereby transforming themselves and learning a new and much better way of thinking, should go on to transform society as well, like science, all the arts, education, warfare, government, and so on.

Dithyrambic Drama is not Entertainment

> If music is to inspire many people to devotion and make them confidants of its highest intentions, the whole pleasure-seeking intercourse with such a sacred art must first be put to an end....

In modern times, we have grown accustomed to seek pleasure as entertainment in art. Nowhere is this most obvious than in our production of movies. But it is also true in the production of ballets, operas, and symphonies.

With dithyrambic drama we have an art form with an

entirely different offering for which the pleasure-seeking audience will find nothing whatsoever. Instead, what he will find is his Self and the long, fearful, and difficult journey along which that discovery proceeds.

> There is no hunger and no satiety, but always only a dull game with the appearance of both, invented for the most vain exhibition in order to mislead the judgment of others about oneself....

People these days engage in art sometimes for no other reason than to attain the appearance of "cultivation," of being cultivated individuals. Imagine how such a person might interact with Nietzsche's dithyrambic drama. They would defile it! And it is for that reason among others that he encrypted it in metaphor: to keep them out. And it worked — for more than a century.

Modern Art Has No Depth, but Dithyrambic Drama Runs Very Deep

As for his mention of art that invokes "satiety and hunger," imagine an individual who finds his Self in Nietzsche's dithyrambic tragedy and his vision of Self invokes a hunger to find a deeper Self, which is precisely what happens. And along the way, the actor must learn to deal with satiety, which becomes a real problem when the actor finds a shallow sense of Self that beguiles him with its beauty and satiates his hunger for a deeper Self. With dithyrambic drama, we have an art form that seriously invokes hunger and satiety. As for the hunger and satiety that other modern art forms invoke, Nietzsche says, by

CHAPTER 5

comparison, it is nonexistent, but people nonetheless boast of it in conversation with others, as when they say "I was so moved.". And the reason they boast of it is to impress upon each other their supposed cultivation by the arts. All of this nonsense is swept aside by the tsunami of originality that dithyrambic drama carries with it.

> As if one feared to perish from oneself through disgust and dullness, one calls upon all evil demons to be driven like game by these hunters: one craves for suffering, anger, hatred, heat, sudden terror, breathless tension, and calls upon the artist as the summoner of this ghost hunt.

He is saying that people, for instance, like to be scared or otherwise excited to escape the boredom of their existence, or worse, the dullness of their souls. And the same thing might be said of people who go to see movies that depict some of the most violent tendencies in human nature. Is what they seek nothing more than an opportunity to waken their sensibilities?

Dithyrambic drama will also awaken your sensibilities but for a purpose. Insofar as the aim of the will to power, which is represented in art by the dithyrambic drama, is more empowerment, which is achieved by a fuller and even fuller apprehension of Self, the subconscious must be integrated into consciousness because therein lies the deepest truest Self, And the only way to incorporate the subconscious is by learning to feel emotion as completely and unreservedly as you did *when you were a child*. Therein lies an awakening unlike any awakening you will ever experience otherwise. But it is for a reason that you strive to achieve this milestone. *There is meaning in the struggle.* And it is to overcome your demons, to redeem them and transform them into angels.

> Art is now in the households of souls of our educated people a completely false or a shameful, degrading need, either a nothing or an evil something.

In comparison to the extraordinary healing powers of dithyrambic drama, there is the art of today, which is either a completely false experience conjured for nothing more than vain reasons or a shameful and degrading indulgence in some of the most base emotions for nothing more than a cheap and very temporary awakening.

Modern Man and the Fear of Self

> The artist, the better and rarer one, is as if preoccupied by a stupefying dream not to see all this, and hesitantly repeats in an uncertain voice ghostly beautiful words which he thinks he hears from far away places but does not hear clearly enough; The artist, on the other hand, who is a modern artist, comes along with complete contempt for the dreamy groping and talking of his nobler comrade, and carries with him the whole yapping pack of coupled passions and atrocities on a rope, in

CHAPTER 5

> order to unleash them on modern man at his desire. For they would rather be hunted, wounded and torn to pieces than live together with themselves in silence. With themselves! - this thought shakes modern souls, this is *their* fear and fear of ghosts.

Obviously, inasmuch as dithyrambic drama represents a journey into the deepest parts of the subconscious and, subsequently, a prolonged and difficult effort to grapple with the knots in which the conscience has become addled therein, learning to live with your Self is a primary requirement to complete the journey. But it is precisely this being alone with oneself that modern man finds so very, very difficult, to say nothing of being alone with the deepest and truest suffering Self, which appears at the outset as something like a haunting ghost because modern man has become so estranged from Self.

Chapter 6

A Critique of Modern Values

Now Nietzsche points out some of the wayward values and even some idiopathy that worsen modern man's lot and make him a bad candidate for the undertaking of dithyrambic drama.

> In the past people looked down with honest nobility on those who traded with money, even if they needed it; they admitted to themselves that every society must have its guts. Now they are the ruling power in the soul of modern mankind, as the most desirable part of it.

That to which we devote all our hopes and desires is achievable only through the exclusion of other potential achievements, which are necessarily deemed lesser and striven toward with lesser devotion.

Who would doubt that, at least where I live in America, the accumulation of even a small measure of wealth is life's most important, most esteemed goal? In contrast, there are some people who might value a

Chapter 6

proximity to Self more highly than *anything* else, especially if there exists a deep and wide gulf between oneself and one's conscience about which one is aware and recognizes the loss. But achieving that proximity requires time and great concentration over a very prolonged period of time. Leisure is a prerequisite of such a lofty goal. And when leisure is not possible, the work towards that goal must be suspended. But when leisure becomes available again, an individual who is truly devoted to his Self will promptly resume the work

If we agree that culture is defined as a mode of thought that aims to heal suffering man, then we should also agree that Self is an integral part of that healing and the mode of thought that guides it. But a culture that does not legislate a desire for Self as a fundamental and integral value fails its people. It makes life difficult for those few who are born with an innate desire for Self and devote their lives to its achievement. And it makes life *impossible* for those who are not born with it and must learn it.

Such is the sorry lot of most modern cultures that teach money as life's highest goal and, above all other things, as its most worthy achievement.

I do intend to disdain wealth nor its pursuit. It is certainly needed for a robust society, for defense and maintenance, and even for the pursuit of lofty goals that require leisure, as is the case with philosophy. But to those who wish to pursue salvation in life, then, aside from the leisure it provides, the pursuit of wealth is wayward. Indeed, I believe there is no more valuable possession in life than Self.

The Pursuit of Self Requires a Protracted and Discerning Effort

He also talks about the value and weight we place on the moment as opposed to more protracted concerns. And he exemplifies this modern value in our use of newspapers, in his day the telegraph, and perhaps in our day cellphones.

> In the past, they warned against nothing more than taking the day, the moment too seriously, and recommended the *nil admirari* and the care for eternal concerns; now only one kind of seriousness remains in the modern soul, it is for the news that the newspaper or telegraph brings. To seize the moment and, to benefit from it, to judge it as soon as possible!

What is important to note about this comment is that the pursuit of Self evolves into the pursuit of the supra-Self. It is not the existing Self in which life celebrates most enthusiastically but rather in the emergence of the deeper Self. And there is always a deeper Self — to a point, after which the absolute transcendence of Self commences the ascension into the supra-conscious. In the course of undertaking Nietzsche's dithyrambic tragedy, the actor is continually plumbing ever deeper depths of the subconscious, integrating into consciousness those deeper emotions, and, through that integration, realizing a deeper and higher Self. Thus, it is important to look beyond the moment, beyond the

CHAPTER 6

existing Self, and not to indulge in the celebratory moment when that deeper Self is realized but instead to value and practice the *nil admirari*.

> One might think that there is only one virtue left in modern man, that of presence of mind. Unfortunately, in truth, it is rather the omnipresence of a dirty insatiable desire and an omnipresent curiosity in everyone.

We are about to learn what he means by "dirty insatiable desire," but, first, we should consider the disadvantage that an "omnipresent curiosity in everyone" or everything presents to life, which, remember, is the will to power or the will to Self.

Nietzsche actually wrote about the problem of being curious about everything in his dithyrambs. Simply put, if an individual is curious about everything he finds within himself, as opposed to paying heed only to that in which he finds his Self, then he will find himself going in all directions, which amounts to no direction, rather than toward that which will reveal his Self. Nietzsche calls it a matter of taste. In the dithyramb entitled "Of the Sublime Men," he wrote:

> Indeed, nor do I like those for whom each thing is good and this world seems the very best. Such types I call the all-complacent.
>
> All-complacency that knows how to taste everything – that is not the best

> taste! I honor the obstinate, choosy tongues and stomachs, which have learned to say "I" and "Yes" and "No."
>
> But chewing and digesting everything – that is truly the swine's style! To always say hee-yaw – only the ass learned that, and whoever is of its spirit! –

In the next paragraph, he points out the more serious problem with the modern psyche in its view of the role that art plays in life. Simply put, as he has already noted, modern man views art either as a source of immediate entertainment or as a pretty dress which he uses to impress his neighbor and to convince his neighbor that he is a better person than one without the cloak of art, without the cloak of cultivation.

> … if it has now acquired all the preciousness of past wisdom and art, and comes in this richest of all garments, it shows an uncanny self-consciousness about its meanness in that it does not need that cloak to warm itself, but only to deceive itself. The need to disguise and hide seems more urgent to him than that of not freezing to death.

CHAPTER 6
Art Heals the Bad Conscience

And Nietzsche views this role that modern man has allotted for art as deplorable insofar as the better role of art in life is that of a healer, which is precisely the role that dithyrambic drama plays. But what specifically needs to be healed?

Without a doubt, it is the bad conscience that truly cultured man endeavors to heal. And it is the success of any culture in this endeavor that is the true judge of its worth, its integrity. *And it is with art that the healing begins and continues afterward.* Therefore, we must get it right.

Nietzsche contends that modern culture uses art not to heal the bad conscience but rather to "euthanize or stun" the bad conscience, to draw modern man into a state of "dullness or intoxication" as a remedy.

> And here the task of modern art becomes clear all at once: dullness or intoxication! Euthanize or stun! To make the conscience not know, in this or the other way! Helping the modern soul to get over the feeling of guilt, not helping it back to innocence! And this at least for a few moments! Defend man from himself by making him silence within himself, by making him unable to hear!

Notice that he cites the phenomenon of getting "back to innocence" as a part of healing. This is a curious notion that helps to understand Nietzsche's idea of healing. He elaborates on it more pointedly in the dithyramb entitled

"Of Chastity" when he says that the will to power does not favor abstinence in the indulgence of the senses but rather innocence in the indulgence of the senses. In other words, if the Self suffers any degradation via an indulgence of sensuality, then the indulgence is bad for the growth of the will to power insofar as it is bad for the Self. Therefore, indulgence can be said to fall within the scope of goodness, specifically with regard to the growth of the will to power, only if it is experienced without an accompanying bad conscience. And that does not mean ignoring the true Self that cried out indignantly in order to experience an undignified indulgence. It is never a good thing to ignore the Self, to become deaf to the Self. Innocence in indulgence means remaining true to one's Self *while* indulging the senses. If, while remaining true to Self, indulgence is a bad experience for Self, move on (see the dithyramb "Of Passing By") to a deeper and higher supra-Self. In other words, what must be indulged is not the passions alone, in and of themselves, but rather a passionate Self. You must always see your Self in your feelings. Otherwise, your experience of passion is outside of your Self, which is not good.

In the above statement, Nietzsche argues that modern art aims to deafen modern man to his true Self, if only temporarily, and to provide him a momentary escape from his true Self. This is important to note because, as we will shortly see, dithyrambic drama drives man ever closer to his true Self, which is antithetical to modern art, according to Nietzsche.

Nietzsche's Invention of the Dithyramb

I now mark for the reader these next few paragraphs

Chapter 6

in the essay as highly significant for their major insights into an understanding of Nietzsche's invention of the New Dithyramb, though none of the insights he articulated are explicit and would, in fact, remain hidden if the reader forgot what I stated at the outset of this reiteration that nothing Nietzsche says in this essay is about Wagner or Wagner's music, but rather it is about Nietzsche and Nietzsche's music, which we know as dithyrambic, or dramatic, music.

> For the few who have only once really felt this most shameful task, this terrible degradation of art, the soul will have become and remain full to the brim of misery and pity: but also of a new overpowering longing. Whoever wanted to liberate art, to restore its unspoiled sanctity, must first have freed himself from the modern soul; only as an innocent person could he find the innocence of art; he has two immense purifications and consecrations to perform. If he were victorious in this, he would speak to the people out of a liberated soul with his liberated art....

"Whoever wanted to liberate art..." is Nietzsche himself. Regarding the liberation of art, at the very least we should understand that he sees a new role for art, specifically in his new dithyramb. And, after reading the above, there should be no doubt in the reader's mind that the role he seeks is that of healer.

He also says in the above comment that whoever

seeks to "liberate" art must first himself have become liberated. That means that Nietzsche has already healed himself and now envisions art, specifically dithyrambic drama, as the means with which to teach others how to heal themselves. And we may rightly surmise that Nietzsche has already healed himself at the time he wrote this essay (1876), or envisioned the entire course of the healing, from beginning to end, with such clarity as to begin teaching it, insofar as we also know that when he wrote *On Moods* (August 1864), at the age of nineteen, he had already begun plumbing the subconscious. (See *The Birth of Dionysia*.) And the fathoming of the subconscious is *the first step* that must be learned (though the learning is also an ongoing process), aside from the initiatory devaluation of the Platonic Self (in "Zarathustra's Prologue"), in the long process of healing that plays out in his dithyrambic tragedy. That is what the drama teaches.

> If he were victorious in this, he would speak to the people out of a liberated soul with his liberated art, and only then would he fall into the greatest danger, into the monstrous struggle; the people would rather tear him and his art apart than allow them to die in shame as they must die before them. It would be possible that the redemption of art, the only ray of hope in modern times, would remain an event for a few lonely souls, while the many could endure looking into

CHAPTER 6

> the flickering and smoking fire of their art: they do not *want* light but glare, they *hate* light - over themselves.

In this, we see that Nietzsche anticipated an unfriendly reaction to his new art form, specifically because it would bring man into a closer proximity with his Self, the "light," and because modern man possesses a strong antipathy toward his Self and the "light." But the reason modern man wishes to avoid his Self is simply because it is wrought with demons that modern man *does not know how to redeem*. But Nietzsche knows. He learned how to redeem his demons in the course of seeking them out. He was driven by a profound *and naturally occurring* affinity for the entire realm of emotion, that which he later referenced as the Dionysian realm, as evidenced by his essay *On Moods*, wherein he reveals that he has already begun its undertaking, at just nineteen! And whatever stood in the way of his Caesarean drive, he conquered. But he conquered it while remaining faithful to the opposite Apollonian drive, the entire realm of myth and idea, instead of becoming a despot, as he also made clear in the preceding statements within this essay. And it was due *entirely* to this faith, that, while giving free rein to the Dionysian realm, he found its redemption in the Apollonian realm. It is for this reason that modern man should not shun or fear Nietzsche's new dithyrambic tragedy: *because it teaches the redemption of demons*. Notwithstanding this new hope, there will be people who will disdain Nietzsche's drama because "they *hate* light — over [and upon] themselves." For those who hate light and cannot move beyond that hatred of light, I know of no other hope except this drama that would help you.

Dithyrambic Drama Requires Mystery and Defies Logic

> So they avoid the new bringer of light; but he goes after them, forced by the love from which he is born and wants to force them. "You *shall* pass through my mysteries", he calls to them, "you need their cleansings and vibrations. Dare for your salvation and for once let the dimly lit piece of nature and life, which you alone seem to know; I lead you into a kingdom that is also real, you yourselves shall say, when you return from my cave to your day, which life is more real and where actually the day where the cave is. Nature is too [so] much richer inwardly, more powerful, more blissful, more terrible; you do not know it as you usually live: learn to become nature yourselves again, and then let yourselves be transformed with and in it through my spells of love and fire.

Here, he speaks effusively about the power of dithyrambic drama. He calls them his mysteries, which is notable for the fact that there are many among the philosophers, who, subscribing to Socrates' overestimation of thought, and especially logical thought, might disdain mystery. And the problem with that is that proto-tragedy and mystery go hand in hand. And there can

CHAPTER 6

be no doubt that proto-tragedy is a highly valuable experience that vastly empowers the individual who undertakes it successfully.

And how is Nietzsche's dithyrambic tragedy a mystery? Simply put, the emergence of the supra-Self from out of the ruins of the existing and collapsing Self, one, defies logic and directly contradicts reality, insofar as reality is defined by Self, which is collapsing in the process, and, two, the emergence of the supra-Self, which is more rightly an artistic creation, appears *out of nowhere*, miraculously and precisely like a mystery, and yet much more "real" than the reality of the old Self.

Continuing with Nietzsche's statements above, he speaks of the "cleansings" that his dithyrambic tragedy provides its actor. And, calling it a "kingdom," he promises "salvation" from within it. He calls that which we know as reality a "dimly lit" version of the more brilliant, more blissful, richer, more natural, and more animated reality that arises out of the supra-Self. He calls the mysterious emergence of the supra-Self profoundly transformative. And when he urges people to "be transformed with and in it [dithyrambic drama] through my spells of love and fire," the "spells of love" refers to the magical enchantment with the vision of Self and with the profound communion with one's inner nature via a true experience with one's emotions. And the "spells ... of fire" refers to the actor's hesitant and wavering but inevitable willingness to experience one's demons, regardless of the fear they invoke, after having found the courage to do so and then found love in Nature within himself.

The question the reader will no doubt ask himself is whether these proclamations are exaggerated or spot-on.

And as one who has undertaken *and completed* his dithyrambic tragedy, as one who has *lived* through his dithyrambic tragedy, I stand alone as his only witness and I proudly attest to his proclamations as, indeed, spot-on. You will rejoice in the collapse of your Self and your Ego and in the emergence of your supra-Self. You will rejoice in your communion with Nature and common sense, especially rare common sense. But you will rejoice most in the transcendence of your deepest and truest Self, beyond the limits of all individuation, wherein your will becomes *absolutely* unfettered and "you fly," as Zarathustra would say.

Music as Will to Self and Power

Finally, in the last paragraph of this chapter (six), he says "It is the voice of *Wagner's art* that speaks to people in this way," but it is really the voice of Nietzsche's new art form, the dithyramb, that speaks to people, as I reiterated above. And then he speaks of "music," as in dithyrambic music, not traditional auditory music.

> His art, seen in the making, is the most magnificent spectacle, however painful that making may have been, for reason, law, purpose, is manifest everywhere. The beholder, in the happiness of this spectacle, will praise this painful becoming itself and consider with pleasure how the primordial nature and talent must turn everything into salvation and profit, however difficult schools it may be,

CHAPTER 6

> how every danger makes it more courageous, every victory makes it more level-headed, how it feeds on poison and misfortune and becomes healthy and strong in the process. The mockery and contradiction of the surrounding world is its attraction and sting; if it gets lost, it comes home with the most wonderful prey of error and lostness; if it sleeps, it "only sleeps with new strength". It steels the body itself and makes it more resilient; it does not feed on life the more it lives; it rules over man like a lively passion and lets him fly just when his foot is tired in the sand, has become sore on the rock.

Once the actor begins to fathom the depths of his subconscious, he discovers his Self. And that is what Nietzsche's dithyrambic tragedy is all about: fathoming dismembered emotions and discovering one's Self in those emotions and then incorporating them into consciousness. And as the actor then embraces his newly-discovered Self (which requires shedding the existing Self, and it is that shedding that constitutes the proto-tragic phenomenon) and continues with his efforts to fathom his subconscious, he goes even deeper and discovers an even deeper sense of Self. And in this whole process, a certain fatefulness comes into play, which Nietzsche memorialized with his "amor fati," by which he meant that learning to love the fate one senses therewith strengthens the will to power that is driving the process and drives it forward. That fatefulness is manifest in the anticipation of the next, aborning Self and in the actor's faithfulness to his will, which exists singularly upon his own deliberation and which he would never abandon after having built. It is in this sense that "reason, law, and purpose" become "manifest everywhere," as stated above in the cited text.

When he says that the "beholder, in the happiness of this spectacle, will praise this painful becoming," it is important to remember that, inasmuch as the dithyrambic actor is himself the beholder of vision in the drama (Self), he is also its object; he experiences powerfully transformative growth. And yet he is also the subject of the drama inasmuch as the drama is a true depiction of human nature. The drama may present gesticulative metaphors that point in a universal way toward demonic suffering, but, when the actor looks for that to which the metaphors point, he finds his *very own demons*. And in the course of his redeeming those demons, he "will praise this painful becoming itself and consider with pleasure how the primordial nature and talent must turn everything into salvation and profit," however difficult his learning and striving may be. Upon approaching every demon, he becomes more courageous. Upon a victory, which results in a clear apprehension of his truer Self, he becomes more level-headed with the common sense that his deeper Self imparts to him. Indeed, via the will to power that drives him forward, he will confront his demons as if feeding "on poison and misfortune and become healthy and strong in the process."

And, even when he loses sight of the way toward his Self, upon returning to its apprehension, still, he finds himself in the company of newly found demonic suffering

CHAPTER 6

that he serendipitously picked up along the way, which he may rightly claim as "the prey of error and lostness." In such a way, self-discovery is ongoing and unrelenting. But if, on occasion, the process of Self-discovery does indeed rest, the actor will emerge from his "sleep" surprisingly more robust and more resilient, because, as he wrote in the dithyramb entitled "Before Sunrise," "the world is deep" and "deeper than day (or consciousness) has ever grasped," which means that things happen within human being beyond the light of consciousness and beyond the sway of the will. Even in "sleep," the actor's spirit and will shall grow, much to the surprise of the actor, and much to his delight. This is what the actor will experience, most certainly. And most remarkably, in the course of confronting his demons, the actor will discover that "his primordial nature and talent" enable him "to fly [above the abyss of suffering] just when his foot is tired in the sand, has become sore on the rock." Indeed, it is only when the will has become most burdened, like the camel carrying the heaviest weight, that the springboard within suffering will summon the will's greatest strength and set him alight like the Phoenix. It is for this reason that Zarathustra (or the will to power) urges the actor to "learn to fly" and "become like the rock."

> Thus the primal nature through which music speaks to the world of appearance is the most mysterious thing under the sun, an abyss in which power and goodness are paired, a bridge between self and non-self.

Dithyrambic Music and Human Nature

In such a way, as I just tried to articulate for you, does dithyrambic music reveal to its actor his primordial nature, to the extent that he is able to apprehend his Self (the "world of appearance") and then experience the dithyrambic music through his Self. And the whole drama of discovery, incorporation, and redeeming is filled with mystery, as when the actor's will awakens from its "sleep" and discovers that he has become stronger and more conscious of his depth, more enabled to *reach* into its depths, despite having exercised no effort whatsoever to do so, though he may subsequently exert tremendous effort. In the course of redeeming his demons by learning "to fly" high above them, specifically high above the principium individuationis, via the springboard that suffering provides, the actor discovers that "power and goodness" are inextricably entwined within the suffering he finds upon entering the abyss in which it resides and is, in fact, "a bridge between self and non-self." It is in this sense that "man is a bridge between animal and superman," between passion and conscience, between raw and wild emotion and Self.

Chapter 7

Dithyrambic Drama as Transport into the Soul of the Dithyrambist

> For it is precisely with this feeling that he takes part in Wagner's most powerful expression of life, the centre of his power, that demonic *transmittability* and self-expression of his nature, which can communicate itself to others in the same way as it communicates other beings to themselves and has its greatness in giving and accepting.

Speaking of Wagner's art but meaning his own dithyrambic art form, Nietzsche speaks of his nature as possessing a "demonic transmittability" and a certain self-expression that can communicate itself to other people *while at the same time* communicating their own nature to themselves, inasmuch as they may be unaware to begin with. When he speaks of transmitting his soul into the soul of another, that might rightly be regarded as demonic, if his soul is evil. But even if his soul is good, it might still be said to be demonic to the extent that it is a communication that goes into the belly of being of the recipient. I think that is the sense in which he means "demonic." But what if the soul that is being transmitted or instilled is messianic? I ask the reader to consider that possibility. What then might be said of such a communication? And quite simply, I would say it should most certainly be considered a most welcome communication. And that is the sum worth of the dithyrambic drama because that is precisely what he has done with this new art form. He instills his own nature into whosoever undertakes his dithyrambic drama. And what is the nature of his soul? It is a nature in which the will to power has become manifest. To be very specific, it is his will that Nietzsche communicates, transmits, and instills with his dithyrambic drama. And it is not a will that acts upon the physical world but rather a will that acts upon the inner spiritual world, the soul, one's Self. And we see that will becoming manifest when he is merely a nineteen-year-old young man, as evidenced in his essay "On Moods," when he writes about plumbing his depths to look for deeper moods.

> If his art allows us to experience everything that a soul experiences when it goes on a journey, when it participates in other souls and their lot, when it learns to look into the world from many eyes, then we can now also, out of such alienation and remoteness, see him ourselves after we have experienced him ourselves.

In this above citation, Nietzsche says exactly what I

just wrote above: that dithyrambic drama allows us to experience everything that Nietzsche experienced as he developed his will to Self, which is the will to power. And I assure you that, once you have completed the drama, once you have run the entire gamut, you, too, will feel as if you have experienced something of the soul of Friedrich Nietzsche. And I would say to you that experience is transmitted via dithyrambic music.

> We then feel it in the most definite way: in Wagner everything visible in the world wants to deepen and internalize itself into the audible and seeks its lost soul; in Wagner everything audible in the world also wants to go out into the light and up into the sky as an apparition for the eye, wants to gain physicality, as it were. His art always leads him down a double path, from a world as a radio play to an enigmatically related world as a play and vice versa; he is constantly forced - and the viewer with him - to translate the visible movement back into soul and primordial life and to see the most hidden weaving of the inner being as an apparition and to clothe it with an illusory body. All this is the essence of the *dithyrambic playwright*, this concept so fully taken that it also includes the actor, poet, musician: just

CHAPTER 7

> as this concept must be taken with necessity from the only perfect appearance of the dithyrambic playwright before Wagner, from Aeschylus and his Greek comrades in art.

"Music" and Appearance as Emotion and Self

The important point here is what he describes as "the essence of *dithyrambic playwright*." In this citation, he goes to his theory of the Apollonian-Dionysian duality when he says "everything visible in the world wants to deepen and internalize itself into the audible and seeks its lost soul" and "everything audible in the world also wants to go out into the light and up into the sky as an apparition for the eye, wants to gain physicality, as it were." Put another way, the Self, which is "everything visible" and represents that which Nietzsche means by Apollonian, wants to see itself in all the emotions, thereby deepening and internalizing itself into the emotions, which Nietzsche equates with "music." And emotions, which represents that which Nietzsche means by Dionysian, want to come into consciousness and become one with the Self, to become a dimension of Self. In such a way, Self, or the Apollonian realm, becomes a reverberation of emotion, the Dionysian realm. And in the same way, Self becomes endowed with much more meaning and power than it would otherwise possess without the attribution of emotion. And via that attribution, emotion is given its freedom, its fullest discharge, which it, too, would not achieve without the attribution of emotion to Self. Thus, the interplay of emotion and Self, of the Dionysian realm and the Apollonian realm, of music and appearance, both benefit from a symbiotic dynamic.

Dithyrambic Drama as Music, Poetry, and Acting

And when Nietzsche writes that "his [Wagner's] art always leads him down a double path," he means that dithyrambic drama always leads the dithyrambist down a double path, that being "from a world as a radio play to an enigmatically related world as a play and vice versa," which R. J. Hollingdale translates alternatively as "from a world as an audible spectacle into a world as a visible spectacle enigmatically related to it." Or to put it another way, the dithyrambist's journey in his writing leads him along a twofold path, that from deep within emotion and then up to a vision of Self that is enigmatically related to that emotion. Except that, being a vision, and an illusory vision at that, Self is never represented in the dithyramb. All that is represented is emotion. The dithyramb is pure "music" and it requires a plausible embodiment. The vision appears only within the mind of the actor and only as a production of dithyrambic drama, only as a successful embodiment of the "music," as myth And insofar as the dithyramb succeeds only when the true emotions that produce the vision are successfully represented and only when the actor succeeds in the embodiment of those emotions does the vision then succeed, then the concept of "dithyrambic drama" encompasses the "musician" who writes the emotions, the actor who embodies it, and the poet who interprets the vision of Self. Interpretation of form (or being) and especially illusory form is always done only by "the poets" or the tendency within us to

Chapter 7

poeticize life. In its strictest sense, Nietzsche viewed poetry as the interpretation of dreams, with dreams encompassing all visionariness, as he stated in the *Birth of Tragedy* when he said "the poet's task is to unmask and read dreams so that the truth in illusion is revealed." In such a way, dithyrambic drama encompasses the actor, the poet, and the musician.

In the remainder of this chapter, Nietzsche continues to write about the dithyrambist and dithyrambic drama and, in doing so, elaborates on the makeup and the influence of dithyrambic drama as well as the motivation and the goal of the dithyrambist.

> If one wanted to connect Wagner's development with such an inner inhibition in a similar way, one might well assume that he had a basic talent for acting which had to refuse to satisfy itself in the next most trivial way and which found its information and salvation in the use of all the arts for a great acting revelation.

Insofar as dithyrambic drama is an entirely new art form, it is notable that Nietzsche proposes a theory on its emergence in Germany in the nineteenth century. He believes it may derive from the extreme importance the Germans placed on music, by which he means traditional audible music. But, more importantly, he also believes it may derive, in the instance of a singular individual, namely Nietzsche, from a desire for a magnificent dramatization of events that could not satisfy itself in the traditional way, which Nietzsche deemed too trivial. Moreover, his desire for dramatization, being grand and not trivial or traditional, encompassed the utilization of other art forms, not just drama but poetry and music as well, and, most importantly, though he does not say it, the production of myth, the greatest of all art forms. In other words, it was not enough for Nietzsche to write a traditional drama because he wanted to write a drama that, upon its undertaking, would draw its actor into itself and lead him to his Self. In such a way, his new dithyrambic art form is, indeed, the most powerful of all the art forms insofar as it imparts redemption and salvation as well to those who partake in it.

The Dithyrambist as Primordial Artist of Actuality

> As one might imagine the development of the primordial dramatist, in its maturity and perfection it is a structure without any inhibitions or gaps: the actually free artist, who cannot help but think in all the arts at the same time, the mediator and reconciler between apparently separate spheres, the restorer of a unity and totality of artistic ability, which cannot be guessed and developed at all, but can only be shown through action.

Notice that he calls the dithyrambist a "primordial dramatist." And that is because the dithyrambist seeks to compose a representation of actuality, which exists beyond the luminescence of reality. Reality is founded on

CHAPTER 7

Self, myth, which is entirely illusory. Actuality is pure "music," pure emotion absent any vision whatsoever. It is all hearing, with nothing that may be "seen." And actuality is the progenitor of reality. Thus, actuality exists beyond the consciousness of reality. Insofar as the dithyrambist composes entirely in "music," he is a "primordial artist."

Self as Mediator and Governor

And the dithyrambist is a "mediator and reconciler between apparently separate spheres" because he composes in "music" and, via the embodiment of that "music," mythopoeia is invoked in the mind of the actor. And in the interplay between the emotions and the creation of Self out of those emotions, we find a mediation and reconciliation between the two realms of that which is Apollonian and that which is Dionysian, insofar as emotion defines Self and, likewise, the creation of Self and the subsequent attribution of emotion to that created Self then gives emotion its greatest freedom. And note also that, while Self gives emotion its greatest freedom by saying "express yourself, but do so only as a dimension of Self, it also provides governance to emotion so that the limits of individuation are preserved during that mighty expression. Suffering results when those limits are violated by titanic emotion, and, therein, the Great Fall begins.

Continuing with the above citation, the dithyrambist seeks to restore "a unity and totality of artistic ability" with the accurate representation of the "music" or emotions that invoke mythopoeia, with the creative act of mythopoeia that arises out of that "music," and then with the poetic interpretation of the created myth, the Self so that the actor learns to view and interpret the inner world of man through the eyes of that new Self. And a drama such as this that employs "music," visionary creativity, and poetry cannot be achieved any other way except through dithyrambic drama, or willful action.

Actuality as a Repudiation of Reality

> But before whom this deed is suddenly done, it will overwhelm him like the most uncanny, most attractive magic: he will suddenly find himself before a power that removes the resistance of reason, yes, that makes everything else in which one has lived up to that point appear unreasonable and incomprehensible: set apart from us, we are swimming in an enigmatic fiery element, no longer understand ourselves, no longer recognize the most familiar things; we have no measure in our hands, everything legal, everything rigid begins to move, everything shines in new colors, speaks to us in new characters....

Here, Nietzsche speaks of his dithyrambic drama as a mystery, and he also speaks of the natural transformation of human nature as it transitions into a way of thinking that is more aligned to nature and more attuned to a theory of life as becoming than the existing mode of thought we use that is badly attuned to a theory

CHAPTER 7

of life as being. For instance, in the course of undertaking his dithyrambic drama (and, at this point, we should clarify that the drama is a tragedy because we will shortly begin discussing that point as well), things will happen that defy logic, such as when the aborning Self rises to the fore and all valuations deriving from the previous collapsing Self — in one moment — fall away as a shedlike outer skin, whereupon entirely new valuations — in the same moment — also come to the fore with their intrinsic bearing as well. In such a moment, the actor will no doubt say to himself, as Zarathustra recalls for him in the dithyramb "Of the Tree on the Mountainside," "My today refutes my yesterday." And in the emergence of that new waking reality, the actor will feel as if everything he has lived up to that point to be unreasonable and incomprehensible. Indeed, a new reality, which is founded upon the new emerging Self, will take hold of him, and everything that seemed previously set in stone, as reality, will fall away, and everything will speak in a new voice and shine in new colors.

> We must be Plato, in order to be able to make up our minds as he does, with this mixture of violent bliss and fear, and to speak to the dramatist: "We want a man who could become all sorts of things and imitate all things as a result of his wisdom, when he comes into our community, to be worshipped as something holy and wonderful, pour ointments over his head and crown it with wool, but seek

> to move him to go into another community.

Fear of the Power of the Dithyramb

If, in fact, Nietzsche's dithyrambic tragedy does indeed lead its actor to his Self — along with all the terrible demons that cast that Self into exile in the first place, and if Nietzsche's dithyrambic tragedy does, indeed, lead the embattled actor beyond his demons, through their redemption, and into a blissful and heavenly existence, perhaps some people will anoint him as the most accomplished artist of all time and then shun his new art form out of fear and therewith deny themselves an experience with human nature that existed only one other time in history, at the dawn of Western civilization. That may happen.

The Dithyramb Does Not Speak to Idealism, only Actuality

> For *we* ourselves have no right to this blindness, whereas Plato, for example, was right to be blind to all that is truly Hellenic, according to the only sight of his eye that he had put into the ideal Hellenic.

And there may be others who are prone to flee from realism into idealism. Those types of people are not likely to find a place for themselves within dithyrambic drama. But for the more realistic people, I can tell you that the future awaits in dithyrambic tragedy.

CHAPTER 7
The Dithyramb as Healer to Suffering Man

> The rest of us need art rather because we have become *seeing* precisely in the *face of the real*; and we need the all-dramatist [i.e., universal dramatist] so that he can free us from the terrible tension for at least hours, which the sighted person now feels between himself and the tasks that have been assigned to him.

But there are others among us who abide by the existence that lives by Self and they became so precisely because they live in the face of reality, who cannot ignore the reality of Self regardless of how terrible that existence may have become through suffering. And those people need the dithyrambist in whose dithyrambs, which speak from the belly of being, everyone may find his Self because his dithyrambs are true representations of universal human nature (thus, Nietzsche's drama is dedicated "For Everyone"). Nietzsche says that those people need art. And by art, he means mythopoeia, the creation of Self.

> With him we climb the highest rungs of feeling and only there do we imagine ourselves once again in the open air and in the realm of freedom; from there we see ourselves and our equals in wrestling, victory and destruction as something sublime and meaningful, as if in enormous reflections of the air; we enjoy the

> rhythm of passion and the sacrifice of it; with every mighty step of the hero we hear the muffled echo of death and understand in its vicinity the highest attraction of life....

Will as Evaluator of Emotion

When he speaks of "the highest rungs of feeling," he implies that some feelings are better than others. But to what end could one feeling be better than another, and in what way could a feeling be better than another? If a goal exists, then there also exist criteria to measure the value of that which assists, even in varying degrees, in the achievement of the goal. And in Nietzsche's dithyrambic drama, the goal is twofold: the production of mythopoeia and the transcendence of the deepest Self to a state in which all the limits of individuated being have been surpassed, which is supra-individuation, what we commonly call genius, but that goal is much more distant than the goal of just finding one's Self. And in that regard, some feelings are indeed more valuable than others. Obviously, those feelings that define Self are more valuable than the wayward and superfluous feelings that derive from Ego. And those feelings — be it a passion, an urge, or an instinct — that contribute to the actor's ability to transcend the limits of individuation, first by looking beyond the horizon of the existing Self and therein to envision the supra-Self, which is purely a tragic vision, and then by summoning and mounting the springboard that inheres in suffering and raises subindividuated man above the black abyss into which he has fallen, then those feelings, urges, instincts, and passions would be the most valuable. Thus, regarding value, there is an hierarchy of feeling. And it is in this regard, that in the dithyramb "Of the Tarantulas," Zarathustra says that "all men are not equal." He is not talking about "men" there; he is talking about passions.

The Value of Tragedy to Life

As the actor ascends into a clear apprehension of Self and then, with the coming forward into consciousness of the demons afflicting that higher Self, succeeds in raising himself above the abyss into which he had previously fallen, he then transcends even that higher Self to a place within his heart and mind in which all the limits of Self, of individuation *itself*, are thrown off, where the will achieves its greatest freedom, which is the "realm of freedom" that Nietzsche cites above. In that state, all the inner battles of conscience and passion that were required to achieve it then appear supremely meaningful. But remember that, in order to achieve the depth of Self in which the defining demons finally present themselves in the clearest reality, many grades of Self had to be shed along the way. And it is the shedding of Self that constitutes the proto-tragic phenomenon. Thus, proto-tragedy also played a very meaningful role in the actor's struggles and victory. Without tragedy, the supra-Self would be impossible. And without the supra-Self, there is no life, or growth. Thus, to life, proto-tragedy is essential and is its most prized possession.

The Dithyrambic Actor as Tragic Hero

In such a way, through his struggles, the actor

becomes a hero and more specifically, a tragic hero. And the individual who has become tragic, who has experienced the need to shed the old Self and, in doing so, has beheld his higher Self, knows that with every step forward the actor must also endure eventual and certain death, but it is a most exhilarating death, if you can imagine such a thing, because it has led directly to a greater apprehension of Self and a freer will. For this reason, Nietzsche writes that "with every mighty step of the hero we hear the muffled echo of death and understand in its vicinity the highest attraction of life...."

What follows in the lengthy remaining paragraph of this chapter 7 is an expose on the nature of the dithyrambist, which is Nietzsche in the course of composing his dithyrambic drama. And what he speaks of in these paragraphs are inner movements of the will through depths and unto heights that few men have achieved before us. And here he is writing about it, except that he writes entirely in metaphor which many people, lacking similar experiences, may find too difficult to grasp.

> Thus transformed into tragic people, we return to life in a strangely consoled mood, with a new sense of security, as if we had now found our way back to the limited and domesticated world from the greatest dangers, riots and ecstasies: To that place where one can travel in a superior, benign and at any rate more distinguished manner than before

CHAPTER 7

> [alternatively translates as: "to where one is considerate-kind and at least more elegant than before"; also, "to those where one can be superior-benevolent and at least superior as a foregone conclusion"]; for everything that appears here as seriousness and need, as a run to a goal, resembles, in comparison with the course we ourselves have taken, even if only in our dreams, only strangely isolated pieces of those all-experiences [universal] of which we are horribly aware; yes, we will fall into danger and be tempted to take life too lightly, precisely because we have grasped it in art with such uncommon seriousness: to quote a word Wagner said about the fate of life.

Tragedy as a Danger to Life that Cures Itself

It is true that, once the actor has experienced proto-tragedy and discovered therewith a deeper and clearer apprehension of Self, he then returns again to the long struggle of finding Self and incorporating demonic feelings into consciousness with a newfound sense of security, as if one has finally learned how to walk even amidst the most tumultuous storms that inner life (and specifically the subconscious) presents. Since great comfort can be found in proto-tragedy, it then becomes a danger, at least with respect to life (as growth) because the beguilement of beautiful Self, which is a direct result of tragedy, stupefies man. By contrast, while the man who has undergone proto-tragedy has seen a higher reality that seems, though illusory, still more true, more awake, and runs more nimbly, the more common reality, to which tragic man inevitably and always descends, quite naturally, after proto-tragedy, appears meaningless and dysfunctional, even in its most serious undertakings. Proto-tragedy *devalues* quotidian reality. It even invokes nausea (fateful resignation of the will) from within the lesser life.

The Birth of Tragedy Out of Dissonance

> For if we, as those who only experience, but do not create, such an art of dithyrambic drama, can almost consider the dream to be truer than the watchful, real thing: how must the creator first assess this contrast! There he himself stands in the midst of all the noisy calls and intrusions of day, life's hardships, society, state - as what? Perhaps as if he were the only one who was awake, the only one who was truly and truly-minded among confused and tormented sleepers, among those who were mad and suffering; sometimes he himself feels as if he were seized by permanent insomnia, as if he had to spend his life, so supernaturally bright and conscious, together with sleepwalkers

> and ghostly serious beings: so that all that which is commonplace to others seems uncanny to him and he feels tempted to face the impression of this apparition with exuberant mockery. But how peculiarly this feeling is crossed when the brightness of his shuddering exuberance is joined by a completely different urge, the longing from the heights into the depths, the loving longing for the earth, for the happiness of togetherness - when he thinks of all this, what he lacks as a lonely creator, as if he should now immediately, like a God descending to earth, "lift up to heaven with fiery arms" everything weak, human, lost, in order to finally find love and no longer worship and, in love, to completely renounce himself!

As I said at the outset of this citation, he speaks here of movements of the inner will with very precise and particular descriptions. And in the last sentence above, he describes his "birth of tragedy from within dissonance" theory.

And as I said a moment ago, proto-tragedy threatens life, one, by providing comfort and satiety with life, and, two, by invoking nausea with life. But then tragedy itself cures the threat it presents, and life goes on. How?

The Will as Music

Quite simply man becomes empowered through his

apprehensions of a deeper Self, that empowerment then leads into a state of satiety, and then that satiety creates a tension and a need for a state in which empowerment is gone in order to eradicate the satiety. This is the state of mind he points to when he says "the longing from the heights into the depths [the subconscious], the loving longing for the earth [for emotion as opposed to image], for the happiness of togetherness [with nature herself.]"

Musically speaking, this is dissonance. And dissonance, or proto-tragedy, directs the actor away from the beguiling Self and, suddenly, the actor says "I can go deeper," partly because he knows *about* the supra-Self, that it exists, partly because he knows there is even greater power in the supra-Self *and he wants that empowerment*, and partly because he has grown tired of the complacency that the beguiling Self imparts and he simply wishes to move again, which is a desire for the will itself, for becoming as opposed to being. But through it all, it is important to remember that the common denominator in all three phenomena is movement, the will, fundamentally as desire — for empowerment.

> But it is precisely the crossroads assumed here that is the real miracle in the soul of the dithyrambic playwright; and if his essence could be grasped by the concept somewhere, it should be at this point. For it is at this point that his art is conceived, when he is drawn into this crossroads of sensations, and when that eerie, exuberant astonishment

CHAPTER 7

> and wonder at the world is coupled with the longing to approach the same world as a lover.

Tragedy as Love of Human Nature

In that moment, when, after discovering and attaining to the supra-Self, human nature literally grows tentacles into the subconscious as if looking for food, and when those tentacles or urges themselves become driven by a passionate love, even lust, for the entire realm of emotion, for more empowerment, that is when Nietzsche discovered his new art form, dithyrambic drama, because he discovered a primary motivation and he knew instinctively that he could depict that motivation as a will.

With his language of feelings, not concept, he thought to direct the reader, who must also become actor, toward his Self and let Nature take over from there because Nietzsche knew what would happen "from there." The actor will experience proto-tragedy, *and the whole process will begin anew*. And each time the actor undergoes the process, his love of inner nature will grow as well, therewith assuring a return to the same process of growth over and over. This is the essence of the dithyrambist's art-making.

Finally, in the last few sentences of this chapter 7, he speaks of the essence of dithyrambic music: its fundamental substance in the sensations and its creativity in myth and idea. But what he says is extremely difficult to follow and discern. Therefore, I will parse it meticulously for the reader's benefit. First, consider the citation.

Tragedy Effects Clairvoyance into Human Nature

His gaze falls down, *clairvoyant and loving-selfish at the same time*: and everything that he now illuminates with this double luminosity of his gaze, nature drives with terrible speed to the discharge of all her powers, to the revelation of her most hidden secrets: and this through *shame*. It is more than an image to say that with that look he surprised nature, that he saw her naked: there she now shamefully wants to escape into her opposites. The hitherto invisible, the inner being saves itself into the sphere of the visible and becomes an apparition; the hitherto only visible flees into the dark sea of sound: *thus nature, by wanting to hide itself, reveals the essence of its opposites*. In an impetuously rhythmic and yet floating dance, in ecstatic gestures, the primordial dramatist speaks of what is happening in him, what is happening in nature now: the dithyramb of his movements is just as much a shuddering understanding, an exuberant looking through, as a loving closeness, a joyful self-expression. The word intoxicatedly

Chapter 7

> follows the course of this rhythm; paired with the word, the melody sounds; and again the melody throws its sparks further into the realm of images and concepts. A dreamlike apparition, similar to the image of nature and its liberator, floats up, it condenses into more human figures, it spreads out in the succession of a whole heroic and high-spirited will, of a blissful downfall and no-more-will: - Thus tragedy is born, life is given its most glorious wisdom, that of tragic thought, and at last the greatest sorcerer and happier of mortals, the dithyrambic playwright, is born.

Speaking of the dithyrambist above, he says that "his gaze falls down, *clairvoyant and loving-selfish at the same time,"* and he is speaking of the individual descending from supra-individuated being into subindividuated being or, more simply, taking a glance into deeper emotions and seeing a deeper Self, beyond the limits of the existing Self, and then reaching out with his will to attain to that deeper Self and bring it to life, which, in the end, turns out to be a higher Self as well, not just a deeper Self. Thus, he experiences a twofold will and glance: one that looks downward into the depths of the subconscious, and one that looks upward toward a vision of his Self *beyond suffering.* And, in that descent and the subsequent, redemptive ascension, he, the dithyrambist, experiences a remarkable illumination of the numerous movements of the will and the effects that those movements produce. In other words, in that tragic descent, the individual sees Nature do its transformative work and literally perform miracles, all before his very eyes.

And he says that, as he looks down into himself and then upward into his mind, he feels clairvoyant, as if he can see all things, especially things that were previously hidden, wherein the entire movement of the will, from beginning to end, is revealed. And in that revelation, the dithyrambist sees the movement that each and every emotion either adds to the will or takes from it, and then he witnesses mythopoeia at the end of the entire, grander movement, whose dominance he had never seen before but now sees clearly. What is important to remember at this point in the essay is that he has already discovered a language in which emotion can be *transmitted* (i.e., entirely without the aid of concept). That is what Nietzsche has already said this far into the essay. Now, with his working experiences, which he just described above, he sees himself as an artist, a composer, a poet, a mystic; he sees himself as the inventor of the dithyramb.

Love of Self as Will to Power

He also says that he feels "loving-selfish" at the same time. Some translators render this phrase as "loving and selfless" and that is an error. I think what is meant by "loving-selfish" is love of Self, and it is a lustful and driving love, not a selfless and passive love. In other words, love of Self is a major component of the will to power. And Nietzsche wrote an entire dithyramb to illuminate the value of love of Self in the dithyramb entitled "Of the Spirit of Gravity."

CHAPTER 7

Next, he goes on to use metaphor to explain the mechanism by which Nature reveals her secrets. In other words, he has anthropomorphized human nature and then ascribed a motivation as a reason for her revealing the things she does. I find his doing this not helpful. But, in any case, he says the reason that Nature gives up her secrets during this deterioration is out of shame. Since Nature, as an anthropomorphized being does not exist, neither does the shame he speaks of. But he is trying to make a point, so let us move to that point because, in fact, he reveals much in it.

Nietzsche's Theory of the Origin of Things in Their Opposite

> It is more than an image to say that with that look he surprised nature, that he saw her naked: there she now shamefully wants to escape into her opposites.

In this citation, he is about to touch on the phenomenon by which things come into being via their opposite. This is an insight that I have seen him mention explicitly only once, and I do not remember where (probably from the notes published in *The Will to Power*). In making the point, as if leading up to it, he mentions the "shame" that Nature feels at being found out as the reason for the transformation. But more practically, the point sheds light on his theory of the Apollonian-Dionysian duality. In other words, upon Nature being seen undressed in raw emotion, she immediately transforms herself into ideation. That is the point he is moving to make, and the metaphor adds a feminine trait to *everything* that is

Apollonian, which would include Self and all ideation.

The Tragic Incorporation of Dismembered Emotion into Self Provides Profound Catharsis

> The hitherto invisible, the inner being saves itself into the sphere of the visible and becomes an apparition; the hitherto only visible flees into the dark sea of sound: *thus nature, by wanting to hide itself, reveals the essence of its opposites*.

First, let me point out that some have translated the last word above, "opposites" as "antithesis," and that is an erroneous translation. He most definitely means "opposites." That which is "invisible" cannot be seen but it can be heard in the sense that emotion that has not been attributed to Self and remains an element of the subconscious can still be perceived (or heard) as a rumbling but cannot be seen as a dimension of Self. Thus, he is referring to emotion — as sound, as music. And that which is only "visible" is ideation, including idea, but especially myth (i.e., mythical Self), in the sense that Self can be a pronounced element of mind but, in its limits of perception, it can still be silent about some deeper emotions. And Nietzsche thought of sensation and ideation as opposites, not merely disparities. Thus, when the dithyrambic actor reaches the deepest point within his subconscious and comes upon raw, demonic emotion, Nature, quite suddenly and quite miraculously, transforms the raw, demonic emotion into ideation. In other words, at that point of fathoming, the actor discovers his truest,

Chapter 7

deepest Self. Conversely, upon attaining that very high apprehension of Self, dismembered emotions that previously played no part in the actor's sense of being, quite suddenly and quite miraculously become liberated as a dimension of the actor's Self, his being, so that he fathoms them finally, so that they can finally be seen and heard, after an eternity of dismembered subindividuation, and his Self attains a profound depth, or, put another way, his idea of Self "flees into the dark sea of sound," again, with "sound" being emotion. And the plunging of the Self into the deep sea of raw emotion is a deeply, deeply cathartic experience to an individual who has previously been unable to feel such deep emotions, regardless of whether those emotions are joy or woe. It is the act of feeling itself that provides the catharsis.

And Nietzsche celebrated that catharsis in his "Hymn to Life," which I now present for your consideration in (three versions) the original German, the translated German, and as my reiteration, which is basically a more liberal translation. First, here is my reiteration.

> Certainly, this is how a friend loves a friend,
> As I love you, mysterious life -
> Whether I rejoiced in you, whether I cried in you,
> Whether you gave me sorrow,
> whether you gave me delight.
>
> I love you along with your happiness and hardship;

> And if you must destroy me,
> I painfully tear myself from your arms,
> As friend tears himself from a friend's breast.
>
> With all my strength I embrace You!
> Let Your flames ignite me,
> And in the throes of battle
> Let me more deeply fathom the mystery in you.
>
> To live and think forever!
> Enclose me in both arms:
> And if you have no more happiness to give me,
> Well then - still you have your sorrow.

Second, here is the literal, strict English translation.

> Certainly, this is how a friend loves a friend,
> As I love thee, enigmatic life -
> Whether I rejoiced in you, whether cried in you,
> Whether you have given me sorrow, whether you have given me delight.
>
> I love you with your happiness and hardship;

CHAPTER 7

> And if you must destroy me,
> I will tear myself from your arms,
> Like a friend to a friend's breast.
>
> With all my strength I embrace You!
> Let Your flames ignite me,
> Let me still in the glow of battle
> Your riddle more deeply fathom.

And here is the original German.

> Gewiß, so liebt ein Freund den Freund,
> Wie ich Dich liebe, rätselvolles Leben!
> Ob ich in Dir gejauchzt, geweint,
> Ob Du mir Leid, ob du mir Lust gegeben.
>
> Ich *liebe* Dich mit Deinem Glück und Harme;
> Und wenn Du mich vernichten mußt,
> Entreiße ich schmerzvoll mich Deinem Arme,
> Gleich wie der Freund der Freundesbrust.
>
> Mit ganzer Kraft umfaß ich Dich!
> Laß Deine Flammen mich entzünden,
> Laß noch in Glut des Kampfes mich
> Dein Rätsel tiefer nur ergründen.

> Jahrtausende zu sein! zu denken!
> Schließ mich in beide Arme ein:
> Hast Du kein Glück mehr mir zu schenken
> Wohlan – noch hast Du Deine Pein.

Also, while the words are officially attributed to Lou Salome, let me go on the record with my belief that these words were most certainly written by Friedrich Nietzsche. There is no doubt of that in my mind.

Mystery is Another Fundamental Component of Tragedy

If the reader would consider my liberal translation, I would point out that two things about life are being celebrated in the text. One is the mystery in life, and the other is the ability to feel, regardless of whether the feeling is joyful or woeful. And when I say "the mystery in life," I mean something that only an individual who has long been separated from his Self and then suddenly finally achieves a proximate communion with Self *precisely* via a newfound ability to feel long dismembered emotions would experience. Specifically, there is a feeling of mystery about the experience. That individual is awestruck by the experience and wonders out loud "what is happening?" And he proclaims further, "whatever this is that is happening within me is very good." And it does not matter whether the feeling is joyful or woeful. What is good is precisely and singularly the ability to feel again, to see one's Self in the depth of Nature within him, in the belly of his being. And it feels — it presents with the countenance of mystery. That is the mystery that the dithyrambic actor *loves* in life; it is the mystery that arises out of a communion with one's own inner nature. Thus, I repeat my point made above that it is the mysterious communion with Self via the experience of feeling that provides the catharsis. *And the catharsis is not possible outside of the apprehension of Self.*

In such a way, sensation induces the production of mythical Self, and ideation enables the mysterious communion with inner Nature, specifically the feelings, via their attribution to mythical Self. And that is the essence of Nietzsche's theory of the Apollonian-Dionysian duality. And that is how Nature, in its desire to hide itself upon discovery by the dithyrambist, according to Nietzsche, "reveals the essence of its opposites."

Summation of Nietzsche's Theory of the Origin of Things in their Opposite

What is important to understand in Nietzsche's citation is that the dithyrambist, namely Nietzsche, has discovered how ideation comes into being and, with it, it also brings sensation into being! That is the point. And that point is especially important when you consider that the inner world of man is strictly a world of becoming. In actuality, there is no being whatsoever. Being, as Self, is something that man himself creates via mythopoeia. That is the art that Nietzsche speaks of in *The Birth of Tragedy*. And it is the creation of being, of Self, that then initiates everything that follows with the ascension of tragic man into the heights of ideation (that which is visible but unheard) and his deepening of the soul into the depths of emotion (that which is heard but not seen), which Nietzsche regards as opposites to each other.

Continuing with the previous, lengthy citation that

began with "His gaze falls down…" in which Nietzsche is writing about the dithyrambist, he now says,

> In an impetuously rhythmic and yet floating dance, in ecstatic gestures, the primordial dramatist speaks of what is happening in him, what is happening in nature now….

Keep in mind that what we are trying to understand in this entire reiteration is precisely the nature and the form of what Nietzsche calls "dithyrambic music" or, more simply, the dithyramb, and more broadly, dithyrambic drama. And in this particular sentence he states explicitly that the dithyrambist "speaks of what is happening in him, what is happening in nature," with "nature" being human nature. In other words, the dithyrambist is speaking about Nature's transformations of natural elements within human nature into their opposites. Specifically, he is depicting the unheard, which is dismembered emotion, into its opposite, which is that which can be seen as a dimension of Self, and the invisible, which is a much deeper apprehension of Self that cannot be seen because it is dismembered from the emotions that define it, into that which can be heard, which is feeling Self.

What I have presented here is a reiteration of Nietzsche's two statements that, one, the dithyrambist has observed Nature's ability to create Self and amplify emotion, and, two, this luminescence is unique to the individual who has achieved supra-individuation and then subsequently descends again into subindividuation. Consequently, that individual, which is Nietzsche himself, has an excellent knowledge of the evolution of subindividuation into supra-individuation. And that is what the dithyrambist, or Nietzsche, depicts in his dithyrambic drama, which is tragic wisdom.

The Dithyramb as a Language of Feeling, Not Concept

Now, how he achieves that depiction is quite another matter. An explanation via concept is not going to succeed. In other words, it would do no good to explain the meaning of life to a young man, who has so little experience with it; he must first gain that experience. Instead of an explanation, what must be done is to the lead the pupil to the gates through which his own willful passing will reveal that meaning in his own terms. And there are many, many gates through which the dithyrambic actor must pass, but it must proceed upon his own will. And "will" is the key word. Thus, the dithyramb depicts will, which is comprised entirely of emotion though it becomes manifest in ideation. And the only way Nietzsche found to depict will was via gesticulative metaphor, which became his "language of feeling" in stark contrast with the traditional language of concept.

Emotion Arises from within Actuality and Reality Arises from within Self

Emotion, unlike Self, resides entirely within the realm of human nature that we call actuality, which is different from the ideational realm of human nature that we call reality, though emotion is just as real or, rather, actual. In fact, reality arises upon the foundation of actuality as a function of mythopoeia and will. Again, the dithyramb is a depiction of will. And while reality does indeed appear within the dithyramb, that is precisely the point, "it appears" — as a vision. All that can be heard, however, is actuality, which is emotion and, specifically, the emotions that comprise the will, the "music."

Completing the above cited statement that Nietzsche made, he says this much more about the dithyrambist:

> ... the dithyramb of his movements is just as much a shuddering understanding, an exuberant looking through, as a loving closeness, a joyful self-expression.

By "movements," he means movements of the will. And he adds that the dithyrambist provides the actor with a "shuddering understanding" of those movements and an "exuberant looking through" or luminescence of those movements. In other words, leave no doubt that the "movements" of the will that are depicted in his eighty-one dithyrambs as *spot-on* depictions of human nature that *anyone* may seek to find within himself. And, with enough effort, upon successfully rendering the gesticulative metaphors in which those movements are represented, the dithyrambic actor will *clearly* hear the will represented therein. Nothing is fictionalized. Everything is actual, or real.

Will as Dithyrambic Music

Then, in the next statement, he begins to speak of the dithyramb as music.

> The word intoxicatedly follows the course of this rhythm; paired with the

CHAPTER 7

> word, the melody sounds; and again the melody throws its sparks further into the realm of images and concepts.

He says, "paired with the word, the melody sounds." If you accept my proposition that the dithyrambist endeavors to compose a representation of the will in his dithyrambs, then here we see that Nietzsche equates will with music because he has "paired" the will with the metaphors in which he depicts the will and he now refers to the pairing as being such with music. And then, as I have reiterated, the will, or the music, "throws its sparks further into the realm of images and concepts." Put another way, will induces mythopoeia, the creation of Self, which is the highest and grandest manifestation of ideation. And beyond mythopoeia, once the Self is created and begins to incorporate the deeper dismembered emotions and the will becomes blocked in that process, then idea and concept become manifest as aids to the will, and those manifestations, as well, are depicted in the dithyrambist's "movements," except that the ideational manifestations of the will cannot be heard by the actor, but only seen, provided the will that begets them has played out within the actor. Otherwise, without enactment, the actor "sees" nothing.

> A dreamlike apparition, similar to the image of nature and its liberator, floats up, it condenses into more human figures, it spreads out in the succession of a whole heroic and high-spirited will, of a blissful downfall and no-more-will....

Self as Image of Nature and as Healer with Illusion

Do not overlook his characterization of the vision of Self that appears to the actor in the dithyramb as "dreamlike." The Self is an illusion, without a doubt. And it is precisely its illusory nature (more specifically, naiveté) that imparts forbearance to the sometimes difficult and titanic emotions that rise up in the course of achieving the communion with one's innermost nature.

Notice also that he says the "dreamlike apparition" resembles nature itself as well as "its liberator.: The liberator is the will. And Zarathustra himself says as much in the dithyramb "Zarathustra's Prologue."

> Everything that feels, suffers in me and is in prison; but my will always comes to me as my liberator and bringer of joy.

> Willing liberates: that is the true teaching of will and liberty – thus Zarathustra teaches it.

And he says that the "dreamlike apparition" is similar to the "image of nature" and the will, which is to say that the Self is indeed a true reflection of one's feelings. One sees the nature of the inner world of emotion, which is entirely cloaked in mystery, in one's Self, and one sees one's will as well in one's Self. In such a way, the Self is unlike static and empty concept. Self is much more than concept; Self is a living entity — that grows! And it is because of that growth that the Self endeavors to see itself in all the emotions, and, when it does, we have spirit, a sense of Self in things everywhere within ourselves. Thus, the otherwise static, unmoving, and rigid ideational Self assumes the nature of emotion and will and becomes fluid and moving. And it may be said that will is the "liberator" insofar as the desire for supra-Self directly effects subsummation of the subconscious, and, once subsumed, those otherwise intolerable emotions become a dimension of Self and, as a dimension of Self, become freer in their discharge, and man says "I feel." Without that feeling experience, emotion remains a haunting, inarticulable, and incomprehensible rumbling of mere "sound," not music.

To put it all more simply, ask yourself which is more natural, the feeling Self or the unfeeling but thinking Ego? Which behaves more naturally and acts or functions more naturally and, thus, more effectively? The answer is obvious. And that naturalness comes from emotion and its incorporation into one's sense of being, one's Self. And that functionality comes from the will, which is lacking in the Ego. The Ego thinks, but the Self feels. And that feeling gives Self life. And that life derives from the incorporation of will and emotion into Self. That is the difference that the nature of the will and its emotions makes.

Mythical Self as Tragic Hero

Notice that he says the "dreamlike apparition," the Self, appears as a succession of an heroic and high-spirited will. To put it another way, it appears as a succession of movements, and those movements, as I clarified just earlier, are the movements of the will — as they are represented in the numerous dithyrambs, with each dithyramb representing a different movement. It is those movements and the confluence that they comprise, which is a will to power, or a will to Self, that eventually become imbued in the Self as emotions, so that demonic suffering is no longer exists as inarticulable and haunting sensations. In such a way, through its own willing, the Self appears as an heroic reflection of one's innermost nature. The Self appears heroic because much has been overcome, conquered, and brought into conformity with the boundaries and severe laws of individuation in its creation.

And he says that the vision of Self that appears as a succession of the will, as its own production and its own creation of art, comes *after* a blissful downfall, that downfall being the collapse of the Self that sat upon the throne before the aborning Self that now overtakes it. And that point goes to the event we call proto-tragedy, which is the most precious, most necessary, and most integral event in the succession of the will toward mythopoeia.

Lastly, in order to explain how Self arises after a blissful downfall and a state of "no-more-will," we need to understand the will to power as a will to Self.

Please note that "no-more-will alternatively translates as "wanting no more." (Hollingdale translates the original German, "Nicht-mehr-Wollens" as "cessation of will.")

Being as a Dangerous Satiety of the Will

The will to power is satiated upon achieving an apprehension of Self. And that says two things. It says that the will to power is a will to Self, inasmuch as its achievement immediately results in satiety. Insofar as an apprehension of Self empowers its beholder, it is in this sense that the will to Self is definitively the will to power. But remember what I said previously that man delights in the exercise of will far more deeply than he delights in the vision of being. Therefore, upon achieving the apprehension of Self, the will becomes satiated and wants no more, and that presents a problem. How does the will move beyond the apprehension of Self if it is satiated?

Tragedy as Dissonance Cures Satiety of the Will

The will moves beyond the apprehension of Self via proto-tragedy. Proto-tragedy saves the will from satiety with even the brightest vision of Self and sends the will to power on its way. And how does proto-tragedy play out?

It is yet another curious phenomenon of Nature that the massive accumulation of power induces a phenomenon which Nietzsche calls musical dissonance. It is that curious phenomenon whereby an ascending melody of booming tone builds to a crescendo and then, quite naturally, descends, through dissonance, into a soft and calm repose wherein a begins anew a fresh crescendo. But how does that play out psychologically?

Genius as the Goal of Life

Quite simply, upon achieving an apprehension of Self, though beguiled by the brilliance and supreme tranquility of that divine moment of apprehension, eventually, somehow, the actor looks beyond the horizon of the very limits of that Self, the limits of its percipience, the limits of individuation itself, *and senses an even deeper mood*, a deeper emotion. And lo and behold, the actor senses a deeper, aborning Self, and the existing Self, which previously so totally beguiled him and cloaked his will in a paralyzing trance of enchantment, *collapses*. *That* is the proto-tragic phenomenon. And that collapse frees the will from that beguilement and invigorates it to start moving again toward an even deeper and even higher apprehension of Self. That is why proto-tragedy is so fundamental and so integral to the process of growth by which the living Self moves beyond its limits, which are definitively the limits of individuation. And that transcendence of limits is how life manifests itself within human being, by definition. Thus, the meaning of life, that toward which it proceeds, is that state of mind that exists beyond the limits of individuation, which is genius, where the will becomes unbounded by those limits of individuation.

Proto-tragedy is a rare phenomenon, just as it is rare for an individual to fathom and then actualize a deeper sense of Self. But that is precisely what dithyrambic drama provides its actor. That is the journey that dithyrambic drama provides by composing a spot-on representation of the will that drives the journey.

Dithyrambic Drama as Teacher of Tragic Thought and Invoker of Mythopoeia

Nietzsche then ends the above citation with the following statement.

> Thus tragedy is born, life is given its most glorious wisdom, that of tragic thought, and at last the greatest sorcerer and happier of mortals, the dithyrambic playwright, is born.

According to this, we should understand that the

work of the dithyrambist is to instill within its actor tragic thought, the ability to think beyond the limits of individuation.

Finally, regarding the above lengthy citation, I wish to illuminate one final point. He says that the image of Self that comes to the actor after a protracted willful effort then "condenses" into a more familiar figure. What he literally says is "A dreamlike apparition, similar to the image of nature and its liberator, floats up, it condenses into more human figures…." What I wish to reiterate is the notion of the Self "condensing" into more human figures.

The Condensation of Supra-Self into Existing Self

When the supra-Self finally precipitates via mythopoeia into a realization, it appears as a very "bright" and effusive instance of ideation whose impression bears down weightily upon the beholder, which is an inner phenomenon that Nietzsche delineates in his dithyrambs as "noontide," though other translators have rendered the word as "midday," but in any case, as a time when the sun appears at its highest point in the sky, meaning that specific moment when the actor achieves the clearest apprehension of Self and at the moment of first discovery.

In another instance that can be found in a note in the *Will To Power*, he speaks of the role that familiarity plays in knowledge and says that there really is no knowledge until that which becomes known also becomes familiar. Upon realizing his supra-Self, the actor does not see any familiarity in the apprehension. He recognizes that what he sees is his Self and there is certainly a measure of familiarity attached to the insight, but there is a much greater measure of familiarity that only comes later, and it is at that later point that the "dreamlike apparition" condenses into a more familiar human figure, wherein the actor recognizes his old Self in the apparition. In other words, while the supra-Self is a new idea, a new myth, that previously lay dormant within the subconscious and is then brought back into life, it really is nothing new; it is the actor's old Self, which he once lived through and then lost to oblivion. Thus, all this willing and creating (mythopoeia) is much like a journey back in time, and nowhere is this "time-travel" more evident than when the actor comes upon his deepest suffering and knows full well, in that moment, that he once was face-to-face with this very same suffering before he repressed it and let it sink into oblivion and therewith began his devolution into Ego a long, long time ago. Only now, with his retrieval, will he chart and traverse a new path with that very same cataclysmic moment of suffering and rise up from the abyss into which it previously exiled him. And it is precisely out of this second encounter that Nietzsche tries to teach the actor the idea of the eternally recurring world, which says that everything that has existed in the past eventually runs anew again, precisely as it ran before, with no variance whatsoever, *but he is talking about events within the subconscious.*

But to return to my point about Nietzsche's statement that the newly-found "dream-like apparition" subsequently "condenses" into a more familiar human figure, it is only after some time has passed beyond the moment of mythopoeia that the actor truly recognizes his old Self in the supra-Self that he has brought into his consciousness. In such a way, there is, in fact, something

Chapter 7

like a condensation into a more familiar human figure. And Nietzsche's mention of this "condensation" in the above citation speaks to his uncanny focus on detail, both here in this comment but especially in his dithyrambs, as well as his strict adherence to the details of that which is real and actual and, thus, perceivable to the reader reading the music *because it also exists within himself*. What the reader should take away from this illumination I just provided is that it is very easy to ignore things that are written in the dithyrambs, but what you are ignoring is rich meaning that serves a useful purpose in your efforts to understand the passion or dilemma he is depicting in that dithyramb. Everything is a clue. Every word that is written is necessary; nothing is extraneous.

Chapter 8

> When the *dominant thought of* his life rose in him, that from the theatre an incomparable effect, the greatest effect of all art could be exerted, it tore his being into the fiercest fermentation.

In the first paragraph, he comments on his discovery that drama ["vom Theater" also translates to "from the drama"] would provide the means with which he could successfully teach everything he had learned about achieving the greatest apprehension of Self along with the greatest emancipation of the will.

> This did not immediately give a clear, light decision about his further desire and action; this thought first appeared almost only in a tempting form, as an expression of that dark personal will, insatiably longing for power and splendor. Effect, incomparable effect - by what? on whom? - that was from then on the restless questioning and searching of his head and heart.

Chapter 8
Dithyrambic Drama Chooses Its Audience

Once he grasped the idea that drama would provide his way to teach, his next question was what to teach and to whom should he teach. And the answers to these two very fundamental questions would define dithyrambic drama and distinguish it from every other existing art form. As it would turn out, the effect he succeeded in producing was the apprehension of Self, or mythopoeia. And insofar as I cannot name a single thing in life or on Earth that is more valuable than the possession of Self, perhaps it is true that Nietzsche has given mankind its greatest gift, as he stated.

Moreover, insofar as the encryption provided by the gesticulative metaphors that are woven in such a way as to falsely but deliberately present a story that makes no sense, then, clearly, his dithyrambic drama chooses who is allowed to enter and benefit from his mythopoeia dithyrambic tragedy. As to what precisely is required to achieve entrance, certainly an ability to look beyond the surface of things is required, just as it is also required, by proto-tragedy, to look beyond the limits of individuation, the horizon of Self. But what is also required is a measure of strict integrity with regard to one's conscience insofar as what is depicted in his dithyrambs are *actual* experiences that play out between conscience and passion. And lastly, given the range of passion toward for which the drama calls the actor to an embodiment, the actor who gains access must be equally capable of the uncommon passions depicted therein. Thus, I believe that foresight, integrity of conscience, and great range of passion are certainly three requirements for anyone wishing to partake in his drama. And I think that answers Nietzsche's questions as to what and to whom he wanted to teach. But in any case, the question he asked "to whom" should he teach resulted in *Thus Spoke Zarathustra* being perhaps the only book in all the world that quite literally *chooses* its audience. Not everyone is welcome. And to be chosen is a distinction and an honor.

Love of Self Equates to Love of Emotions

> Each further stage in Wagner's development is marked by the fact that the two basic forces of his being become ever more closely united: the shyness of the one before the other diminishes, the higher self from then on no longer begrudges the more violent earthly brother with its service, it loves him and must serve him.

This statement goes directly to Nietzsche's theory that art arises out of an agon-driven, evolutionary interplay between the two realms of the Apollonian and the Dionysian, or, rather, that art as mythopoeia, the creation of Self, arises out of a contentious, power-grabbing interplay between sensation and ideation. And he says that, by the time he discovered his idea that drama could provide him the means with which to teach his philosophy, within his own soul, there was much less of an antagonism between his Self and his feelings, that he had discovered the life that arises within him when he embraced his feelings. He celebrates how that embrace brightens and emboldens his vision of Self and frees emotions that are otherwise imprisoned within him.

CHAPTER 8

> When the goal in this development [evolution] is reached, the most tender and purest is finally also contained in the most powerful, the impetuous impulse goes its course as before, but on other paths, to where the higher self is at home; and again this descends to earth and recognizes in all earthly things its likeness.

The Naturalization of Man

Regarding the agon-driven evolution between emotion and Self, when its goal is reached, that goal being a dissolution or enfeeblement of the antagonism so that the two realms of emotion and Self unite into a partnership, then "the most tender and purest" elements of static and eternal Self may be found within the most raw, most titanic, most exigent elements of transient emotion, as if opposites have united via a miraculous and redemptory phenomenon. In such a moment of union, a man who was previously tormented by haunting demons, suddenly proclaims "I feel my pain" and rejoices in his calm yet disturbed predicament. Such a man, thereafter, has achieved a measure of freedom (and power) that allows his emotions to achieve the discharge they demand, while, at the same time, allowing the antithetical and ideated Self to exist alongside it. And, after that reconciliation, the Self now descends into the deep and previously unfathomable realm of emotions (metaphorically, "the sea") and sees itself in that antithetical and emotional depth. *What a curious and most mysterious turnaround!* Nietzsche calls this turnaround the "naturalization" of man.

Finally, in this, the eighth chapter of *Richard Wagner in Bayreuth*, we find Nietzsche's reason for calling his representation of the will to Self, which is the will to power, music or dramatic music, which we will call dithyrambic music. And he states his reason in the first sentence of the third paragraph.

Regarding the question for whom Nietzsche the dithyrambist should write his dithyrambic drama, he concluded that he would write it for "the people," by which he did not mean the peasantry or poor folk, *but rather those whose ruth in life placed them near his heart.* People whom he viewed as people after his heart.

> ... if a multitude suffered the same misery as he did, that would be the people, he said to himself. And where the same need would lead to the same urge and desire, the same kind of satisfaction would have to be sought, the same happiness would have to be found in that satisfaction.

Dithyrambic Music as Melos

The next question to be asked is what "same misery" did he find that "the people" and he himself suffered with? And the answer is subindividuation: the loss of Self, which happens to anyone who suffers but happens most egregiously to those who suffer most egregiously, by which I specifically mean the victims of crime who survive.

He predicted that the loss of Self via suffering and

CHAPTER 8

the resultant state of subindividuation would create the same overriding and ruling need in anyone who suffered subindividuation as well as the same urge and desire arising out of that need, and, as it turns out, the confluence of that same need, urge, and desire is a will to Self, which, given the empowerment that is imparted by Self, defines the will to power. He predicted that the same satisfaction, namely an apprehension of Self, would become manifest in all the people suffering that same need *as a consequence of that need* and that the same happiness would be found in that satisfaction for those who, indeed, became satisfied by that remedial apprehension of Self.

The same need that creates the same urges and desires, and the same satisfaction that meets that need and those urges and desires (the will), and the same happiness that becomes manifest in that satisfaction — constitutes a *melos*, a meaningful continuity of feeling in which one feeling (be it a need or a satisfaction of that need) *necessarily leads into another as a succession*, just like a melody. And it is that melos that defines dithyrambic music. It is also that melos that defines meaning in life. Thus, Dionysian life is deeply meaningful.

Moreover, insofar as urges and desires are emotional and thereby transient, unlike idea or concept that are both intransient, and insofar as it is precisely those urges and desires that most fundamentally drive the whole movement toward the apprehension of Self, that movement being the will, while ideation plays a less fundamental and more supportive role, then rhythm comes into play as an economic consideration in the need to utilize the emotions that comprise the will more wisely and frugally. And the economic role of rhythm in the genesis of the will adds to the musical character of the will to power. In fact, I should add, Nietzsche wrote an entire dithyramb on this consideration of an economy in passion, and it is called "Of Voluntary Death," in which he teaches self-terminating the "run" or duration that a passion is allowed to experience in order to preserve its vigor and especially the hope it lends *even in its end*, which is a preservation that would certainly add to that same passion on its next "run," thus also preserving a certain rhythm.

Regarding the composition of dithyrambic music, as opposed to its reading (or rendering) and practice, which is a completely different area of study that I already covered extensively and in depth in *The Birth of Dionysia*, the theory stated above in this preceding paragraph is comprehensive and complete — about composition.

It should also be pointed out that while the dithyrambs represent the various movements and events of the will to Self (power), some dithyrambs represent inner circumstances that arise directly from subindividuated nature and stand as a hindrance to the development of the will to Self, and those dithyrambs do not rightly represent movements comprising events arising out of the will to Self but, instead, represent naturally (or unnaturally) occurring forces of human nature that must be undone or negated, weeded out, which is why the dithyrambist includes them in the drama.

Life as the Will to Power

Before moving on to the next point in the essay, I should also like to point out that the melos Nietzsche has discovered in the will to Self, insofar as it is a true and *actual* representation and insofar as it is a spot-on

Chapter 8

delineation of how life manifests itself within human being, then it also restores meaning to life. And the restoration of meaning to life is a milestone in the history of Occidental culture. And there should be no doubt that the will to Self is indeed a spot-on delineation of life within human being. Self is the being in human being. And it is precisely the role that proto-tragedy plays in that process of growth, whereby the limits of Self are extended beyond itself to an even greater depth and greater height, that singlehandedly defines life itself. Wherever we see a living being extended the limits of its being, there we may rightly say that life is playing out, by definition.

> When he now looked around for that which comforted him most deeply in his distress and raised him up, what would meet his distress most soulfully, then he was conscious with the consoling certainty that this was only the myth and the music, the myth which he knew as the product and language of the people's distress....

The Psychology of Self Becomes the Mythopoeia of Self

Next, he goes on to write specifically about myth and "music" as that which may most effectively address the great need out of which "the people's" distress, which is subindividuation, arises most fundamentally. In other words, myth is Self, and music is the fundamental need for Self as well as the urges and desires arising out of that need and moving toward an apprehension of Self, the confluence of which is what we call will. But now, with the words myth and music, he has brought the discussion of Self and will out of the science of psychology and into the realm of art.

> How did myth and music live in our modern society, as long as they had not fallen victim to it? A similar fate had befallen them, a testimony to their mysterious togetherness: The myth was deeply humiliated and distorted, turned into a "fairy tale", into a playfully delightful possession for the children and women of the stunted people, completely stripped of its wonderful, serious and holy male nature....

Dead Myth Versus Living Myth

What is important to understand in this statement is that Nietzsche viewed myth as something in human existence that plays a robust, most esteemed, and very effective role in life and especially art. But in our modern times, myth has become something far less than itself. We view myth as a false notion of cause, something that was once held as truth but which has since become disproven, such as the ancient belief that a multitude of gods drove the phenomena that occur around us but which we moderns now understand as a foolish and totally incorrect notion. In place of mythical gods, we now believe in forces of nature as the cause of all phenomena around us. But that is the difference between living myth and dead myth. Gravity, for instance, is, in fact, a myth, but, being a living myth, it is something we hold as truth, as real. A myth is a construction of the mind that enables interpretation of phenomena and being a part of the mind places it in the realm of ideation, far from the realm of emotion. And without interpretation, there is no life. But when a myth fails as a method of interpretation, then it dies; there is actually a death in the sense that the failed myth is remembered. When a myth fails and dies, it becomes merely a false notion of cause. Unfortunately, modern man's entire view of myth is that of a false notion. *And that is a shortcoming that cannot be overstated.* Modern man has no concept of myth that includes the magically creative capacity of myth because Nietzsche was the first to demonstrate it in the dithyramb. A concept of dithyrambic music would help in that deficiency.

> Here the artist clearly heard the command that was given to him alone - to bring the myth back into the masculine and to disenchant the music, to make it speak: he felt his power for *drama* suddenly unleashed, his dominion over a yet undiscovered middle kingdom between myth and music established.

Genius in the Restoration of Myth

Insofar as Nietzsche clearly considered himself an artist, he thought of restoring the power of myth to its glory as his highest aim. And when he says that he wanted to find a way for myth "to speak," he meant that he wanted to find a way to "communicate," or, even better, "transmit" the power of myth, which is what he did with dithyrambic drama. When it came to teaching, Nietzsche did not "proffer concept" as a means nearly as much as he "transmitted instinct."

Myth as the Middle Ground

He speaks of "his dominion over a yet undiscovered middle kingdom between myth and music established...." Quite simply, he is saying that he has discovered a new art form, a new way of transmitting knowledge, to say nothing of what he has done for life itself. And he specifies myth and music as the two most important points of that "middle kingdom." Notice that he does not say "upper" or "higher" kingdom, but rather, specifically, "middle kingdom." And the "middle" he speaks of, which is that place begotten *only* of tragedy, exists between the two realms of sensation and ideation, *in a balance*, but a balance that is dynamic and creative, not static and unchanging. Remember what he said in the *Birth of Tragedy*, that tragedy is the result of a union, a reconciliation, between the Apollonian and Dionysian worlds.

Dithyrambic Myth is Natural

Finally, regarding the value of myth and its relation to the equally valuable "music," Self is a living myth. And to say that Self is a myth is *not* to say that it is not real. Quite the contrary, to call something a living myth, as opposed to a dying myth, is precisely to grant it the color of reality. But its reality is rooted deeply in feeling, in emotion, in the entire Dionysian realm of the duality. That is the relation between idea and feeling, between myth and music. The music, or emotion, produces the myth, or

CHAPTER 8

Self. But to reach that inner "middle" point within one's own soul wherein the reconciliation exists is a major achievement. It does not come naturally. As far as I know, it only comes from this man's art, but it is nonetheless most natural; I can tell you that, with my experience.

> His new work of art, in which he brought together all that was powerful, effective and blessed that he knew, he now put before the people with his great and painfully incisive *question*: "Where are you, who suffer and need as I do? Where is the multitude which I as a people long for? I will recognize you by the fact that you should have the same happiness, the same consolation in common with me: your joy should reveal your suffering to me!

At this point, quite presciently, Nietzsche makes predictions about how people will react to his dithyrambic drama. First, he looks to those people who "suffer and need" as he does.

> But how did he feel? Nobody gave an answer, nobody understood the question. Not that one remained silent at all, on the contrary, one answered a thousand questions that he had not even asked, one chirped about the new works of art as if they were actually created to be talked about.

And he finds no listeners. None. Instead, he finds only people who can find no more to do with his new art form than to talk it to pieces. And I ask you, the reader, *is that not precisely what has happened?* And for more than a century now in 2021.

> Wagner [Nietzsche] was as if stunned; his question was not understood, his need not felt, his work of art looked like a message to the deaf and blind, his people like a fantasy; he staggered and swayed. The possibility of a complete overthrow of all things appears before his eyes, he is no longer frightened by this possibility: perhaps beyond the upheaval and devastation there is a new hope to be found, perhaps not - and in any case the nothing is better than the disgusting something. He was soon a political refugee and in misery.

A Radical Departure from Traditional Form

What follows in the remainder of this and the next, much longer paragraph is an account of his coming to realize that no one is going to understand his dithyrambic drama and that its destiny and fruition lay solely in the future. Thereafter, Nietzsche resigned himself to writing for a species of man that did not yet exist in nineteenth century Europe. And with that, he took liberty to do things his way, regardless of the difficulty it imposed on those

CHAPTER 8

who did not understand what he was trying to do with his new art form.

> His work would not have been finished, would not have been finished, if he had only entrusted it to posterity as a silent score; he had to publicly show and teach the most inexplicable, the most reserved to him, the new style for his performance, his presentation, to set the example that no other could give, and thus to establish a *style tradition* that is not inscribed in signs on paper but in effects on human souls.

Clearly, it would have helped Nietzsche to advance his cause, to at least quicken acceptance and perhaps the practice of his new art form, if he had provided a demonstration of its rendition and practice. But he never did that — either because he ran out of time after succumbing to the final stage of his illness shortly after finishing 'Zarathustra and never spoke again or because he chose to entrust it *entirely* to posterity. I believe the latter. But in the above statement, we see that he understood the need for a demonstration of his new art form and worried that his masterpiece would remain too obscure to survive, let alone flourish.

Chapter 9

The Dithyramb as Real Experience

> If art is only the ability to communicate to others what one has experienced, then every work of art contradicts itself if it cannot make itself understood: The greatness of Wagner [Nietzsche], the artist, must consist precisely in that demonic *communicability of* his nature which speaks of itself in all languages, as it were, and reveals the innermost experience with the greatest clarity...

From the above statement, we should take Nietzsche's understanding of art to entail the communication of one's own experiences. And that is an important point because it means that the experiences depicted in his dithyrambic drama, some of which are extreme and not easily achieved, are plausible and indeed achievable, inasmuch as he himself already undertook them.

His comment that his art form, dithyrambic drama,

reveals the "innermost experience" attests to the fact that what is depicted is not a story of characters but rather something much, much deeper: the will and all the actions and manifestations it undergoes in the course of its development toward an apprehension of Self.

And the fact that he says the dithyramb speaks of the "innermost experiences" "in all languages" goes to the nature of dithyrambic music, which, just like traditional audible music, speaks to everyone via a universal language *of feeling*, not concept.

> ... his appearance in the history of the arts resembles a volcanic eruption of the entire undivided artistic capacity of nature itself, after mankind had become accustomed to the sight of the separation of the arts as if it were a rule.

The Multiple Talents of the Dithyramb

It is Nietzsche whose appearance in the history of arts marks a milestone because his invention of dithyrambic drama comprises the coming together of many art forms into one, especially mythopoeia, which is a purely natural phenomenon that constitutes the single greatest manifestation of art within human being itself, within the soul, not in any physical worldly form like most other art forms, but rather within the souls of its actors.

Specifically, in addition to mythopoeia, dithyrambic drama employs poetry, whose beauty is reflected not in rhyme but in poignancy. It employs drama in the embodiment of its poetic metaphors and in the willful action that those embodiments lead the actor into. And it employs music in the mellifluent and advantageous timing of the passions that comprise that will.

Dithyrambic drama is not like, for instance, Homeric storytelling, which employs poetry alone. It is not like a Shakespearean tragedy that employs poetry and drama but not music. And it is not like one of Beethoven's symphonies that employs music but not poetry or drama. Dithyrambic drama employs all three art forms: poetry, drama, and music, though the music is not traditional audible music but music in a more fundamental form. But it is the production of myth within the human mind, mythopoeia, that qualifies dithyrambic drama as art more than any other aspect of it.

> One can therefore vacillate as to which name one should attach to it, whether it should be called poet or artist or musician, whether each word should be taken in an extraordinary expansion of its concept, or whether a new word should first be created for it.

I propose that a new word be proposed as a reference to what Nietzsche created in *Thus Spoke Zarathustra*. Let us call it a dithyrambic drama and, more specifically, a dithyrambic tragedy. Let us call the text in which it is composed dithyrambic music. And let us reference the individual who undertakes Nietzsche's dithyrambic tragedy as a dithyrambic actor.

> The *poetic aspect* of Wagner is shown in the fact that he thinks in visible and

CHAPTER 9

> tangible processes, not in concepts, that is, that he thinks mythically, just as the people have always thought.

Mythical Thought Is Not Conceptual Thought

We need to understand what Nietzsche means by thinking mythically, or thinking "in visible and tangible processes," as opposed to thinking in concepts. We already know what it means to think conceptually. If you read a simple statement like "the man walked up the stairs," you conceptualize a man, the process of walking, and a staircase. If the simple statement is changed to 'the man walked up the stairs carrying a scepter," and if you have no concept of "scepter" because you have never seen one or never had the concept explained to you, then you cannot conceptualize the statement. Eventually, you learn the concept somewhere, and then the statement makes sense. But the full rendition requires all the concepts that are used. That is how people read and it is how they talk. The words that are read or heard reference a concept, which the listener or reader conceptualizes in their mind.

But the dithyramb does not use words or anything else to reference concepts; the dithyramb does not reference concept. In a dithyramb, the words constitute dithyrambic music which means they reference an inner state of mind, whether that state of mind is founded on a passion or a belief. The fact that the music is written in gesticulative metaphor means that the metaphors point to the state of mind as clues to the particulars of the state of mind. Thus, each word has particular meaning. And the long introspective process of decrypting those clues directly leads the actor *within himself* to the particular state of mind that is being called by the dithyrambist, whereupon the actor proclaims "I see the analogy" between the metaphors and the passion or the belief. Then, after embodying the passion or belief so that the actor becomes *driven or compelled* by it, through music, the actor also "sees" or "hears" within himself another passion or belief arising *out of it*. Thus, the dithyrambist who composed the dithyramb that the actor struggles to decrypt and embody must be able to think in terms of those passions, those various state of mind, just as the conceptual thinker requires all the concepts being used in conceptual thought. But concept never enters into the process of rendering a dithyramb, neither in the writer's composition nor in the actor's enactment. It is not concept that is referenced. Most often, what is referenced is a feeling, something that moves the will, although sometimes what is referenced is a state of mind arising out of a belief that may obstruct it, in which case the actor must not seek to embody something but rather he must eradicate or weaken something, usually a belief.

> The myth is not based on a thought, as the children of an artificial culture think, but it is itself a thought; it communicates an idea of the world, but in the sequence of events, actions and sufferings.

CHAPTER 9

> The Ring of the Nibelung is an immense system of thought without the conceptual form of thought.

Is Not Founded on a Single Thought

In order to understand this comment, let us take Self as an example of a myth. And then we must understand how myth is considered to be either something arising out a single thought or is itself a whole system of thought, a way of thinking unto itself.

One of the most difficult tasks in life is finding a way of interpreting it. Self provides that interpretability. And the postulation of Self is triggered by what I call the mythopoeic instinct, which is exemplified in animals who see something in their midst move and immediately believe that the moving thing is a living creature, such as we see in cats who observe a ball of anything rolling across the floor and start chasing it. It is the movement itself that triggers the instinct to postulate a living being as the cause of the movement. The key word is "movement." When man perceives movement, whether as part of the inner world or the outer world, he cannot think otherwise but to predicate the movement *to something* as its cause. It works the same way within man; he senses movement within himself, such as emotion, and he postulates a living being as its cause. And he calls that being Self.

Descartes celebrated the mythopoeic instinct with his famous axiom, the cogito, "I think, therefore I am." According to Descartes' axiom, just thinking about the origin of thought would trigger the mythopoeic instinct within an individual and, voilà, he or she would have an idea of Self with which to understand the inner world within. That is an example of a myth based upon a single thought, with, in this instance, the single thought being the origin of thought. In other words, the individual thinks to himself "where is my thought coming from; what makes me think?" And the answer he gets is "because I exist; I am something, a being; that's where my thinking comes from. How could anything come out of me, let alone reasoned thought, if there was not something within me producing it? Therefore, I exist." However, it must be noted that Descartes postulation was of the Ego, which is different from the postulation of Self. And the difference is the difference between mythical thought that is founded on a series of events and mythical thought, like Descartes' that is founded on a single event. Though both are myths, the Ego is a substantially less powerful myth, insofar as it imparts much less manageability of the inner world than does Self. And manageability is just as important as interpretability.

Unlike Ego, Self arises from mythopoeia that is triggered by feelings, not thoughts. And, when even deeper feelings are discovered, so, too, does the idea of Self deepen. In fact, the whole process of fathoming the Self via the fathoming of feeling leads through a lengthy succession of gradations of Self. In the beginning, all one perceives is the simple idea of Self, only later does a *sense* of Self develop. And only after the sense of Self arises does there then arise an actual vision of one's Self, and then its voice, and finally its spirit. And the best moment does not finally come until that spirit achieves freedom, so that the Self, without fear, sees itself everywhere and in everything, which is precisely what the Self wants, as the champion of interpretability. But that only comes, as I said, after considerable growth which is itself driven by courage and the newfound ability to fathom ever deeper feelings. In such a way, mythical Self is a "sequence of events, actions and sufferings." Mythical Self is not founded upon a single thought but rather a series of events. And while both Ego and Self communicate an idea of the world, the idea that Self communicates extends to a far deeper and more sophisticated world than that which is communicated by Ego. In fact, true Self plumbs so deeply and becomes so real that it becomes itself a progenitor of thought, with that thought reflecting, or reverberating, the depths and the common sense to which that Self has extended itself into the depths of the belly of being. In such a way, Descartes' Ego is founded on a single thought (I think, therefore I am), but Self is founded on a succession of feelings extended ever deeper into the world and which, itself, prompts a way of thinking about the inner world. And it is a way of thinking arising out of experience and the instincts that played out through those experiences.

Myth is Founded in Feelings

Finally, regarding the last statement in the above citation about *The Ring of the Nibelung*, it is rather about *Thus Spoke Zarathustra* that Nietzsche says it "is an immense system of thought without the conceptual form of thought." Insofar as the dithyramb is a representation of the will, in all its various movements, and dithyrambic drama is, overall, a representation of the will's development toward the apprehension of Self, and insofar as the will is comprised entirely of emotion as its base and ethos, or belief and idea, only in its sustenance, then

Nietzsche's dithyrambic tragedy is a journey geared toward myth, which arises out of feelings, not concepts.

> Perhaps a philosopher could put something very similar to it, something without any image or action, which would speak to us only in terms: then the same thing would be represented in two disparate spheres, one for the people and one for the opposition of the people, the theoretical man.

Explaining the Dithyramb and Living the Dithyramb

In a curious twist of fate, while I was the first person to learn how to read Nietzsche's dithyrambic music and how to practice it, therewith becoming the first person not only to undertake his dithyrambic drama but to complete it also, I am also the only one to provide an explanation of the journey toward supra-individuation *in concept*, whereas Nietzsche taught it through feeling and instinct. But if supra-individuation is achievable only via will and not concept, for what purpose would I have written this conceptual explanation? Simply to show that the journey exists and that it is precisely what is depicted in his dithyrambic tragedy. Knowing that the journey exists, that it is worthwhile, and that it can be achieved via Nietzsche's *Thus Spoke Zarathustra*, hopefully, will encourage people to undertake it. That is why I present this conceptualization.

CHAPTER 9
The Dithyrambic Drama Blocks Entrance to Theoretical Man

Lastly, notice his reference above to "the people" as something that is antithetical to the "theoretical man." This reference should give us some idea of "the people," "the folk" he sought for his dithyrambic drama, as mentioned in the earlier citation. "The people" are those individuals who are able to think mythically unlike "theoretical man" who endeavors to understand everything conceptually, and by "mythically," I mean in terms of one's feelings — intuitively, not theoretically or conceptually. For Nietzsche, "the people" is the person who has chosen to live life listening to and abiding by what his conscience tells him., in opposition to a person who does not. That type of person is the "folk" in Nietzsche's dithyrambic tragedy, and it is only that type of person, who lives life according to his conscience, that can understand dithyrambic music. Other types, any other types, cannot understand it.

> Wagner does not address this person, for the theoretical man understands the poetic, the myth, only as much as a deaf man understands music, that is to say, both see a movement that seems senseless to them.

At the very least, we should take this statement to mean that *Thus Spoke Zarathustra* does not address itself to everyone. In fact, it addresses itself only to "the people," "the folk," by which, we now understand, is any individual who has the ability to endeavor to understand something intuitively instead of merely conceptually.

Again, insofar as the dithyramb is a representation of the will's movements and insofar as the will is comprised entirely of emotion, then the dithyramb requires an intuitive understanding. A conceptual understanding of the emotions that comprise the will would be an intellectual comprehension that would impart none of the *movement* that inheres in emotion and comprises will. But it is will that the dithyramb is written to communicate.

Coincidentally, Nietzsche's dithyrambic drama does indeed provide a conceptual representation, which presents itself as a story about a character named Zarathustra and his travels. But, as it turns out, that false countenance was a deliberately deceptive trick that was meant to lure "theoretical man" away from the drama so that he might never touch upon the real meaning and then defile it. And does that false story not seem "senseless" to them, despite all their desperate efforts to render it sensibly? Indeed, it does.

> From one of these disparate spheres one cannot look into the other: as long as one is under the spell of the poet, one thinks with him as if one were only a feeling, seeing and hearing being; the conclusions one draws are the connections between the processes one sees, that is, actual causalities, not logical ones.

Dithyrambic Drama Requires Initiation

The two spheres he references are the poetic (or the musical) and the theoretical (or the conceptual), between which he sees an antithesis. Those who normally rely on a conceptual understanding of things will read *Thus Spoke Zarathustra* as a story and they will see (or hear) nothing of "the music," the will, in the text. Those who rely on an intuitive understanding of the text will see the text as gesticulative metaphor and they will actively and diligently look for meaning in those metaphors. And the meaning they will find is the will that is being pointed to, which they can only find within themselves. Then, upon finding that will, whether it be a raw passion or a circumstance of passion and conscience, they will embody it. Upon embodiment, the dithyramb will then show "the actor" what the dithyrambist found in it, specifically, with an eye toward developing the will and moving toward a greater apprehension of Self. And that continuing growth of the will is also depicted in the dithyramb as metaphor and is only discoverable as an offshoot (further along the course of development) of the *earlier* embodied passion or circumstance, as music, as will. As such, a conceptual reader will see nothing. Or, to put it another way, the dithyramb can only be understood by an initiate.

Tragedy as Naïve Mysticism

Also, when he says that the "connections between the processes [or events] one sees," he is referring to the passion and conscience in the dithyrambic depiction as well as the offshoot that develops out of it later as will. And that "connection" does not appear in the actor's mind or belly as a logical conclusion but rather as an intuitive leap that, quite the contrary, given the nature of mysticism, sometimes defies logic. *But it happens nonetheless* because it is actuality and not reality. And that is how dithyrambic drama achieves its mystical magic. In fact, it is only upon the events occurring within the realm of actuality, like mythopoeia, that reality later arises, as when the actor sees a deeper and higher apprehension of Self, which then precipitates a deeper and higher sense of reality, all of which is an illusion, though a necessary illusion, unlike actuality, which is much more "real" than reality in its lacking of that naiveté, and naiveté is the key and most influential element of illusion. Naïveté, just like tragedy, makes life happen. Without both, life is impossible.

> If the heroes and gods of such mythical dramas, as Wagner composed them, are now also to make themselves clear in words,|413| then there is no more obvious danger than that this *literal language* awakens the theoretical man in us and thereby lifts us up into another, unmythical sphere: so that in the end we would not have understood more clearly through the word what was going on before us, but would not have understood anything at all.

> Wagner therefore forced language back into a primordial state, where it almost does not yet think in terms, where it is still itself poetry, image and feeling…

Chapter 9

This is yet another definition, in Nietzsche's own words, of dramatic music, of dithyrambic music: "language [forced] back into a primordial state, where it almost does not yet think in terms [or concepts or logic], where it is still itself poetry, image and feeling...." I put the emphasis here on "feeling." The text in which *Thus Spoke Zarathustra* is written points to feelings that we can all find within ourselves. Those words do not point to concepts — of anything.

Dithyrambic Transport as Teacher

Could Nietzsche have written text that accurately describes emotion and then instructed the actor to find it within himself and then embody it? Perhaps. But what he did instead was to use metaphor to point to it and then *force* the actor, who wants to render the metaphor and make sense of it, to find the same feeling within himself to the point wherein he proclaims "I see the analogy." Upon that proclamation, the actor has isolated the pathos within himself, and it is only with that isolate that he may then take hold of it and properly embody it and look for the offshoot of the will that emerges from it and then properly mount that offshoot, that will, that music. The better way to assure that the embodiment will be achieved is to force the reader into the lengthy, introspective process of rendering those metaphors. That process presents a far more robust outcome than what may have occurred with text that conceptually depicted emotion.

However, Nietzsche did not tell anyone this was what he had done; he did not tell people how to read the text. In fact, he went in the opposite direction of explaining what he had done and actually led people into a complete and utter misunderstanding of what he had written, deliberately and in a calculated way. And as a result of his strategy, people have not "understood anything at all."

> In general, one could say of Wagner, the *musician*, that he has given a language to everything in nature that until now did not want to *speak*: he does not believe that there must be something dumb. He also immerses himself in dawn, forest, fog, crevice, mountain heights, night showers, moonshine and notices a secret desire in them: they also want to sound. When the philosopher says it is *a* will that thirsts for existence in animate and inanimate nature, the musician adds: and this will wants, at all levels, a sounding existence.

Dithyrambic Drama and Poetry

Insofar as the dithyrambist is engaged in the production of myth, which is a process that goes more deeply into human nature than any other artist has ever before gone in order to achieve his art, then it may be rightly presumed that processes which make that production happen will have to be represented amongst the numerous movements of the will. And in that representation, it may also be said that those movements are given a voice and made to speak — by the dithyrambist — about their way of working, their way of influencing. For instance, the dithyramb "Of the Sublime

CHAPTER 9

Men" speaks of the very strong antipathy that exists between demonic suffering and Self or Ego. In order to defeat that antipathy and bring demonic suffering into consciousness, it is necessary to see that the fear of the subconscious that the antipathy generates within the actor is actually *a delusion*, that, on the contrary, the incorporation of subliminal suffering into consciousness does not destroy the individual, which is precisely what the delusory ventriloquism proclaims, but rather it heals him, magically. (That, by the way, is a good example of how the will to Self and power defies logic.) These things, specifically the delusory ventriloquism that is presented by the Ego's antipathy toward the subconscious, have never before been brought to the light. In such a way, things within nature that had previously never "spoken" now speak, which calls poetry into the dithyramb. But, in fact, there are many things afoot within human nature, in all the various movements of the will, that the dithyrambist sheds light on, and they are all made to reveal the secrets of their way of influence specifically with regard to the will to power, to show whether they hinder it or grow it.

> In order to reproduce the great curved arc of a passion, he really found a new means: he took individual points of their trajectory and indicated them with the greatest certainty, in order to then let the listener *guess* from them the whole line. From the outside, the new form was like a compilation of several pieces of sound, each of which seemed to represent an insistent state,

> but in reality a moment in the dramatic course of the passion.

Dithyrambic Drama as Cultivation of the Will

Taking "individual points of [the] trajectory" of a "great curved arc of a passion [the will to Self and power]" is exactly what Nietzsche has done with his dithyrambs, as I have already explained numerous times above. Each dithyramb is a representation of a movement of the will. Sometimes that movement is toward an apprehension of Self, which means the movement must be cultivated. And sometimes the movement is away from an apprehension of the Self, which means it must un-learned and extirpated.

Ultimately, the goal in Nietzsche's dithyrambic drama is not just the greatest, deepest, and brightest apprehension of Self but rather transcendence of that greatest apprehension. What is ultimately celebrated in dithyrambic tragedy is not the gradations of Self, the luminescent and complacent beauty of being, but rather the will and especially its freedom from the limits of individuation, with that freedom constituting supra-individuation. And that goal is not always clear in the various movements, most of which point to the Self and its achievement. Instead, the actor must eventually perceive by his own accord, by his own will, that supra-individuation, or the transcendence of the truest and deepest Self, is the actual goal of the will. And there is a dithyramb, "Of the Thousand and One Goals," that explicitly speaks to this point, this goal.

CHAPTER 9

> ... it is precisely the demand that one has something very specific to say and that one says it in the clearest possible way that becomes all the more indispensable the higher, more difficult and more demanding a genre is.
>
> Therefore, Wagner's entire struggle was to find all the means that would serve *clarity*; above all, he needed to free himself from all the biases and demands of the older music of the states and to give his music, the resounding process of feeling and passion, a completely unambiguous speech.

On the Poignancy of the Dithyramb

On the one hand, given the metaphorical nature of the text in which dithyrambic music is written, the text of *Thus Spoke Zarathustra* can be totally misleading, as when the reader proceeds as if reading a story and resorts to conceptual reading. On the other hand, even when the reader is reading his feelings into the text and truly "listening" to "the music," then again, for the same reason due to the use of metaphors, the text can be very unclear and confusing. But when the actor finally finds the passion that is represented in a particular dithyramb and isolates it within his own inner being, he finds the nuances therein, which are also represented in the dithyramb, crystal clear. It is quite remarkable how precisely and in a detailed manner Nietzsche has written his dithyrambs. For instance, in one dithyramb, as the actor approaches his most fearsome demons, Zarathustra says that there is no going back at this point because the vaulted subconscious has been broken through and can no longer be tamed or repressed. It is extraordinary to experience a thought that is written down in the dithyramb and for the dithyrambist to have predicted that the actor would experience that particular thought in that particular circumstance, but that is the nature of dithyrambic music, wherein, due to the inherent melos, one thing always leads to another. But even more important is for the reader to note how easy it would be to overlook this particular aphorism about the inevitability of the approaching demon. And yet, when the actor considers it for a good amount of time, what he realizes is the need to understand that inevitability and fate are afoot here, because inevitability and the fatefulness *add to the will*. That is why the dithyrambist pointed them out in the dithyramb, and he may have done it in only a single aphorism. Thus, the dithyrambist writes with extraordinary detail and in the clearest measure, which may easily be overlooked and missed. And in every instance where the dithyrambist writes, he writes something that is meant to add to the will's development, whether that addition is achieved through cultivating something or weeding something out.

> Wagner grasps every degree and colour of feeling with the greatest firmness and determination; he takes the most delicate, remote and wildest movement in his hand without fear of

> losing it, and holds it like something hard and solid, even if everyone else should see in it an unassailable butterfly. His music is never vague, atmospheric; everything that speaks through it, man or nature, has a strictly individualized passion; storm and fire take on the compelling force of a personal will.

I think this comment confirms everything I just said above. It is important that the actor heed every aphorism in every dithyramb because there is value in each of them.

The Dithyramb is Transformative and Redemptive

> Wagner's music as a whole is an image of the world as it was understood by the great Ephesian philosopher, as a harmony which the dispute bears witness to, as the unity of justice and enmity. I admire the possibility of calculating from a plurality of passions, which run in different directions, the great line of an overall passion: that such a thing is possible is proven to me by every single act of Wagner's drama, which tells the individual stories of different individuals and the overall story of all of them side by side. We feel it already at the beginning that we have before us reluctant individual

> currents, but also, powerful over all, a
> current with a mighty direction....

With three statements, Nietzsche makes three different points above, all with regard to the dithyramb and dithyrambic drama.

In the first, he says that dithyrambic drama is an image of the inner world of man, and it is an image with deep enmity and deep justice, with a glorious harmony appearing right alongside the horrific dispute from which it came into being, all rolled into one. And we see that image of justice and enmity in the existence of demonic suffering that flows hidden within the subconscious but also existing alongside the Self which cannot look upon that suffering. Where might we find more enmity if not in that intractable and wholly insurmountable conflict? But what happens? The actor eventually finds his deeper Self in that suffering and brings the suffering into consciousness, therewith closing behind him the vaulted subconscious wherein that suffering can no longer flee into oblivion. So now he must live with that suffering. And what happens next? He finds the springboard that inheres in that suffering, which only comes after exerting a great tension upon the will. Then, upon mounting that springboard, he rises above the principium individuationis, so that he is no longer in Schopenhauer's trusty rowboat sitting atop the sea of emotion but rather *above it*, as if flying but certainly weightless, and then he ascends into the white abyss that exists above the black abyss, like remedial spots on the eye after looking into the horror of existence. Given that scenario, I ask you, where is there more justice than in that transcendence and that ascension? Therein lies a world in which the greatest injustice and the greatest justice lie eternally entwined. In such a way does the will move beyond insuperable obstacles. In such a way do things come into this world *out of their opposites*.

The Dithyramb and the Over-Self, the Übermensch

In the next statement, he speaks of "the possibility of calculating from a plurality of passions, which run in different directions, the great line of an overall passion...." This is precisely his formula for the dithyramb and dithyrambic drama. Each dithyramb depicts a movement of the will. Some of those movements bring the actor into the depths of his subconscious, wherein he must fight demonic suffering. Other dithyrambs bring him into the heights of the supra-conscious, wherein he realizes a greater apprehension of Self. But, given the nature of proto-tragedy, no sooner as he ascended into the heights of a greater apprehension that he then finds himself again delving into the depths of the subconscious, wherein he finds himself delving ever deeper and deeper. And that is what the dithyrambs teach him: to go into different directions — at the same time, into the subconscious and into the supra-conscious. And through it all, an overriding will comes into focus. And it is a will that drives him beyond the limits of the highest apprehension of Self, beyond the limits of all individuation — into supra-individuation, wherein anything that might fetter the will is thrown off completely, allowing it absolute freedom.

Chapter 10

> He is driven by the deepest need to establish for his art the *tradition of a style* through which his work, in its purest form, can live on from one time to another until it reaches that *future* for which it was predestined by its creator.

The "tradition of a style," through which Nietzsche's work, *Thus Spoke Zarathustra*, is meant to survive in its purest form from one generation to the next is the cryptic metaphorical text in which it is written. And do not overlook his mention that he never intended for his contemporaries to understand his dithyrambic drama and that he wrote it for a type of man that did not yet exist. Is that not exactly what happened more than a century after the publication of *Thus Spoke Zarathustra*, when the "tradition of style" was finally decrypted and the drama was first undertaken by someone?

> Wagner possesses an insatiable urge to communicate everything that relates to the foundation of his style and, in this way, to the continuity of

CHAPTER 10

> his art. To make his work, to quote Schopenhauer, as a sacred deposit and the true fruit of his existence, to make it the property of mankind, to lay it down for a better-judging posterity, this became his purpose, which takes precedence over *all other purposes* and for which he wears the crown of thorns, which was once to become a laurel wreath: On the safeguarding of his work his striving was as resolutely concentrated as that of the insect, in its last form, on the safeguarding of its eggs and provision for the brood, whose existence it never experiences: it deposits the eggs where, as it knows for certain, it will one day find life and food, and dies in safety.

Insights into the Legacy of Dithyrambic Drama

In the first statement above, Nietzsche seems to be saying that it is important for him to explain how his new art form works so that people can begin to benefit from it. But he never explained anything, perhaps because his time ran out, given the progression of whatever ailment it was that eventually left him in a non-cognitive state for the remaining *ten years* of his life. However, I think it is more likely that he left it to one person who would eventually figure it all out and then carry the torch for him, which is precisely what happened, though it took a very long time to pass that torch.

In any case, what he says next in the above statement

is quite prescient. Given the transparency in the statement, I do not think it needs any reiteration, but for those who may harbor any doubts, I offer one anyway.

To make *Thus Spoke Zarathustra* as a sacred deposit and true fruit of his existence, to make it the property of mankind, its greatest gift, to lay it down for a better-judging posterity, this became his purpose, which took precedence over all other purposes and for which he wore the crown of thorns that would become his laurel wreath, He was as resolutely focused on the safeguarding of *Thus Spoke Zarathustra* as is the insect, in its last stage of life, on the safeguarding of its eggs and provision of its brood, whose existence it will never know; it deposits its eggs where it knows they will one day find food and life and it dies contented.

> His art is not to embark on the barge of written records, as the philosopher is able to do: art wants the *able-bodied* as transmitters, not letters and notes.

The Dithyrambic Actor Becomes a Work of Art

From this, quite simply, we are meant to understand that *Thus Spoke Zarathustra* is not an explanation of anything that requires some manner of conceptual comprehension. Quite the contrary, what is required with this work is an *undertaking*, a performance — because *Thus Spoke Zarathustra* is a drama, specifically a dithyrambic drama, and dithyrambic drama requires acting out. The actor must learn to embody the will that is represented in gesticulative metaphor and then allow himself to become driven by that will along the journey that it drives. And the journey it drives him through is a journey into the subconscious, wherein he discovers his Self. Then, as he delves even deeper, specifically via tragedy, he achieves an even deeper apprehension of his Self. And all of this graduated mythopoeia is the work of art as it plays out in human nature, and it is very capably depicted in dithyrambic drama. In such a way, the actor becomes himself a work of art.

The Dithyramb Teaches Instinct

No manner or measure of explanation will impel the actor to confront his most haunting demons. What is needed for that is a desire for Self that eventually grows into a passionate love for Self — and a passionate love of Self specifically for the empowerment that Self imparts, which is nothing less than a lust for power. Thus, it is not reasoning that will drive the actor into a confrontation with his demons; the actor needs instincts and passions. And that is what all the many dithyrambs teach as the various movements of the will. In such a way does dithyrambic drama impress itself upon the actor and teach him— in passion and deed, not with explanation.

> His writings have nothing canonical or strict: the canon lies in the works. They are attempts to comprehend the instinct that drove him to his works and, as it were, to look himself in the eye; once he has succeeded in transforming his instinct into knowledge, he hopes that the opposite process will take place in the souls of

> his readers: this is the prospect with
> which he writes.

In the first statement above, he mentions canon and the fact that dithyrambic music does not teach canon. There are numerous dithyrambs in *Thus Spoke Zarathustra* that imply canon is being taught, such as we see in "On War and Warriors," "On Chastity," "On the Friend," "On Science," and numerous others. None of them teach canon. All of them represent and teach movements of the will. The gesticulative metaphors in which they are written are the only manner of textual representation that a dithyrambist is able to use in order to point the actor toward the passion that the dithyrambist wants him to embody. And embodiment of passion is the first step in dithyrambic drama. The metaphors are mere clues that point the actor in the general direction. The clues are always spot-on but they are mere clues. And they are cloaked in cryptic metaphor that deliberately leads the reader into a story. It is the process of unravelling the cloak that actually *transports* the actor *within himself* into the passion via a lengthy introspection that requires a careful examination of all the passions so that, in the end, he looks himself in the eye, or, to put it another way, he comes face to face with his conscience. In such a way does the dithyrambist represent instinct and passion in sophisticated metaphor, so that the actor may then do the reverse and transform that knowledge into living instinct and passion.

And if the dithyrambist took an opportunity to use his cryptic metaphors in such a way as to distract the dawdling reader and everyone else he chose to keep out of the drama, well, then, we have to admit that the

CHAPTER 10

dithyrambist is one very astute and skillful writer. But there is no explicit canon being taught in *Thus Spoke Zarathustra* in the same way that one reads it in the bible. That is not to say, however, that rules and demands or laws of nature are not indeed being taught; they are. But those laws of human nature are revealed only in the instincts and passions themselves and in their interplay, by living through them, via the actor's own will, not via word or concept.

Chapter 11

> ... how do these sentences sound to our ears: that passion is better than stoicism and hypocrisy, that honesty, even in evil, is better than losing oneself to the morality of tradition [custom], that free man can be both good and evil, but that the unfree man is a disgrace to nature and has no share in any heavenly or earthly consolation; finally, that everyone who wants to become free must become free through himself, and that freedom does not fall into the lap of anyone as a miraculous gift.

True Freedom Comes from Within

Regarding the above statement, let us start with the last part, as to how one becomes free. Without a doubt, the freedom he speaks of is freedom from the grip of one's demons; that goes back to his theory of the bad conscience in *The Genealogy of Morals*. Thus, to want freedom is to want to find it within oneself, not outside oneself, with, for instance, the freedom that wealth brings in temporal life. True freedom occurs within oneself. Moreover, it does not fall from heaven like a gift from God. It is something you must work to achieve. And sometimes you must work your entire life to achieve it. (I strongly recommend starting with *Thus Spoke Zarathustra*, preferably in your twenties, if not sooner.)

The Reason We Suffer

If there is such a thing as Nature and if it acts upon us with a will, perhaps a man who suffers will have asked himself "why do I suffer so egregiously?" That question is tantamount to asking "why has Nature put me in this terrible lot?" And the answer is that Nature has made suffering man a promise, if you believe that Nature has a will and an intent. "Redeem the suffering I have inflicted upon you," she says, "and you will enter into a paradise that others who do not suffer will never even imagine." That is the promise that Life has made to man. Those who suffer without dedicating themselves to work to redeem their suffering are a disgrace to Nature insofar as they ignore Nature and the promise she has made to them, and they are undeserving of any good thing that comes their way via Nature, so argues Nietzsche.

A Natural and an Unnatural Way of Life

And finally, in the first part of the above statement, regarding the two ways to go through life, one being natural and the other unnatural, a spot-on example of that would be a life driven by a will to Self, which is the way to one's suffering and its redemption, and a life driven by morale and everything that follows from morale, especially from its sublimated form, like self-righteousness and the banishment of suffering, or one's demons. The latter would be the way away from one's suffering, which would be unnatural. Of the two, one is filled with hope and meaning, and one is utterly hopeless and devoid of meaning, which would be morality. And the only thing that makes a difference in which choice is made is integrity of Self or honesty toward one's Self. And that is what Nietzsche meant when he said "that honesty, even in evil [or suffering], is better than losing oneself to the morality of tradition." Ultimately, it is love of Self, and even a lust for the empowerment it brings, that drives life most effectively onward through its later stages when satiety has become a problem and tragedy becomes a possibility. Morality does precisely the opposite. And morality is unnatural.

> Now, however, true satisfactions and salvations exist only for nature, not for unnaturalness and false sensation. Unnature, once it has become conscious of itself, is left only with a longing for nothingness; nature, on the other hand, desires transformation through love: it *does not* want to be, it wants to be *different*.

Morality Versus Tragedy as a Way of Life

Regarding the consolation that Nature provides and the consolation that morality provides, let us compare the two. In relation to suffering, the illusion of Self provides a way to look upon one's demons if the actor truly finds his Self in that suffering because it imparts delight in

CHAPTER 11

visionariness. Who has not felt as if haunted by one's demons and, as a haunting, perceived an absolutely insurmountable obstacle in moving forward past that suffering, whether it be deep pain, humiliation, or fear? But as soon as the actor sees his Self in the insurmountable emotion, then it suddenly and quite miraculously becomes not only tolerable but incorporable into consciousness as well, as a dimension of being, as an emotion rather than a faceless and unspeaking haunting. Quite suddenly, the condemnatory nature of a haunting demon is transformed with the naiveté imparted by the visionary Self. And once into consciousness, it stops receding again into the oblivion of the subconscious so that it becomes a mandate for action. And what action does the actor eventually find? He finds the springboard that inheres in all suffering and, mounting that springboard, he ascends out of the black abyss into which his suffering compelled him and into the white abyss, which you, the reader, may be unaware until you experience redemption; but I assure you it exists as one of those very rare things that originates in its opposite and can only be found in its opposite. This is the meaning of the axiom that says the way to heaven is through hell. That is redemption, and that is salvation. And it is achievable only through a confrontation with one's own inner demons. If the dithyrambic actor succeeds in this confrontation, the resulting freedom is quite extraordinary; it even enters the spirit.

A Definition of Morality

Morality, on the other hand, teaches a very different route in life. Morality teaches that the way out of misery is to mount morale or, even better, righteousness. And then, when morale becomes sublimated (in the same way that sexual lust sublimates into spiritual love) so that it enters the spirit, everything that demoralizes human being becomes banished according to the new values dictated by the spirit, where spirit is the herald in life, the guide that directs the will. And what is antithetical to morale? Demonic (or dismembered) suffering and all other instances of suffering.

A Condemnation of Morality

There is true satisfaction in finding one's Self in a haunting demon. And there is true salvation in mounting the springboard that suffering (and only suffering) provides as a way into the supra-conscious, where that haunting demon is redeemed. This is the way of Nature's creativity. But there is no true satisfaction or true salvation along the path that morality takes man. There is only the peace of a calm sea because suffering has been banished. And even though suffering still exists, as in the subconscious, through morality, one has become numb to it and certainly deaf to it. Nietzsche asserts that there is something unnatural in that deafness toward oneself. And he asserts further that the true nature of human being includes the Dionysian realm, necessarily. In the end, when these two modes of thought have run their course, on the Dionysian side, we have the creation of the supra-Self and the total emancipation of the will in the transcendence of individuation, but on the morality side we have just a dreary, enfeebled, and monotone existence founded on a peaceful inner calm that seeks above all to preserve itself and banish all manner of disturbance. Nietzsche claims that the will has lost its way in morality

CHAPTER 11

because life itself wants nothing more than to become something more than what it already is, to be creative. And for that reason, as well as the fact that morality has banished half of human nature from the domain of being, he condemns morality and all moral thought.

The Will Wants Becoming, Not Being

When Nietzsche says that Nature wants to be "different," he means that Nature wants to become, as opposed to merely being. Nowhere is this more evident than in tragic man, who has learned to look beyond the horizon of an existing Self, to see ever more deeply into the subconscious, and to extend the limits of consciousness into that depth, thereby growing the vision of Self. That is what the will wants. It does not want to be complacent in the beguiling beauty of Self. It wants to become — more willing.

> And now ask yourselves, you generations of now living people! Was this written *for you*? Do you have the courage to point with your hand to the stars of this whole heavenly vault of beauty and goodness and to say: it is *our* life that Wagner placed among the stars?

Nietzsche's Legacy: The Birth of Dionysia

Now ask yourselves, those who read this reiteration. You know now that dithyrambic drama is a journey into the subconscious and then beyond it into the redemptive supra-conscious. But none of it is a work of fancy or fantasy. Rather, it is the work of life, which may require a lifetime to complete. And each step proceeds only upon courage. It is deeply meaningful and deeply rewarding. And there is a measure of rebirth in it that makes the rebirth which the Christians claim — a caricature of odd nature.

Having said that, the reader should ask himself if this journey has been chartered for him. Does he have the courage to undertake it? And does he see his own fate in it?

> He who asks in this way, and asks in vain, will have to look for the future; and if his gaze should discover in some distant place just that "people" which is allowed to read its own history from the signs of Wagner's art, he will ultimately also understand *what Wagner will be to this people*: - something which he cannot be to all of us, namely not the seer of a future, as he might like to appear to us, but interpreter and transfiguration of a past.

We may take this statement to mean that Nietzsche foresaw a culture of people arising out of his dithyrambic drama in the future, which goes to the point that I have made in *The Birth of Dionysia* that he founded a new culture, which will be called Dionysia. And most certainly, those people will see Nietzsche as "the seer of a future." But to those among us today, at least we should understand that Nietzsche has succeeded in finding a way

CHAPTER 11

to incorporate the subconscious into life and then redeeming it, which is no small task. And best of all is that he found a way to chart that journey and enable others to undertake it themselves. That is the best of all.

In Summary

Dithyrambic music is the intuitive language of feelings, and especially instinct, in which one good conscience *speaks* to another, thereby transmitting from one soul to another feelings and instincts pertaining to the good conscience, but without using concept as a vehicle of transmission. That is my concept of dithyrambic music. I was the first to discover it, and I have been practicing it for fifty years now.

If I said that the text in which *Thus Spoke Zarathustra* is written is a literary representation of the will, that would be much easier to understand than if I said that the text is dithyrambic music, which it is. The concept of dithyrambic music is a difficult concept to grasp. It is a highly rarified concept. But it is not necessary to have a concept of dithyrambic music in order to begin reading *Thus Spoke Zarathustra*. All that is necessary to do that is an understanding that it is written in metaphor, that the metaphors require rendition, that rendition requires a protracted introspective process during which that which is pointed to by the metaphors is actually found within oneself, and then, once isolated and delimited and thereby embodied, the reader becomes actor as he employs that which he has learned to develop his own will. And the most important embodiment is that of an instinct that the

In Summary

dithyrambist specifically wants the actor to learn. None of that requires a concept of dithyrambic music to be successful.

Why, then, do I highlight the idea and dedicate an entire book to its articulation? Because, rarified though it is, it is an idea to which only Nietzsche attained and succeeded, though he never celebrated the idea in the same measure that he celebrated all his other ideas, and also because it goes to the nature of the will to power and reveals much about its way, its development. It is, in fact, so rare a concept, that Nietzsche mentions it explicitly only once, in the Second Preface to *The Birth of Tragedy*, when he says "From music? Music and tragedy? The Greeks and dramatic music?" And with no elaboration whatsoever, it is very easy to presume he meant music that is used to dramatize, as an accompaniment, rather than what he actually meant, which is music that must be acted out. But music cannot be acted out. Will, however, most certainly can be acted out. And will is what he really meant. But he called it dramatic music. Thus, I believe it is important to know what it is about the will to power that is musical.

Moreover, virtually every reference to "music" that Nietzsche makes throughout all his writings, with only a handful of exceptions, is a reference to dramatic music, which, again, is will. Thus, a concept of dithyrambic music would be very helpful to anyone wishing to understand Nietzsche's writings about music and about will as well.

And an explanation of the concept "dithyrambic music" begins with an explanation of the human will. At its simplest, absent the idea that the text is dithyrambic music, the text in which *Thus Spoke Zarathustra* is written is a literary representation of the human will. In the case of Nietzsche's dithyrambic drama, the will that is represented is a will to Self. And insofar as an apprehension of Self, which is graduated, empowers its beholder, the will to Self is also a will to power.

And what is will?

On one day, the will to Self may be a desire for Self. On another day, it may be a youthful hope to reclaim Self from the ravages of suffering. On a third day, it may be an inkling that Self exists in some mood one senses lingering under the surface of discerning consciousness. And on yet another day, it may be a vision of one's Self emerging from within the chaos of thought and emotion within oneself, But, in *every* instance, it is fundamentally a *desire* for Self in whatever form it may be found, and it is that desire that effects *movement* toward one's Self. That movement is attributable only to will, and that is my concept of will. Will does not arise within human being in a frenzied moment; it is cultivated. And insofar as it may take a different form in different moments, it is essentially a confluence of movements and efforts, not just one effort. And Nietzsche's dithyrambs depict those various movements. And that confluence, or that will, is what most resembles music, especially music that leads to an acting out within oneself as a yearning for Self.

Keep in mind that, upon discovering one's Self in this or that subconscious emotion and then riding the emotion to its natural outcome, which will likely be an experience of pain or humiliation or fear upon one's Self, the "ride," being emotional as it is, will be quite moving, which is a characteristic of music, simply. And along the way, there will very likely be obstacles that prevent the

IN SUMMARY

beholder from completing the "ride" to its natural outcome, such as a lack of courage, which will result in a lull. All of this moving forward and backward, this wax and wane, is an experience that Nietzsche equates with music. And in the end, when the "ride" succeeds in reaching its end and the beholder "sees" his Self again after a very long time spent away from it, that, too, Nietzsche equates with the same visionariness one experiences under the influence of traditional, auditory music, which prompt what he calls "daydreams" in *The Birth of Tragedy*. But, in any case, the attainment of visionariness and the resulting vision of Self, which is myth, *creates a huge problem* in the continuation of the longer melody, beyond Self, because there is a longer journey, which Nietzsche calls "Übermensch," or over-Self. The will does not seek myth as repose; the will seeks everlasting willing, for the wax and wane to never end. Thus, the attainment of Self becomes a problem.

Throughout the multitude of dilemmas between passion and conscience, throughout all the willing that ensues from reading *and practicing* Nietzsche's dithyrambic music, the essential experience is reducible to a singular joyful experience in the act of willing, by which I mean a confluence of various and sometimes discordant passions and conflicts that inevitably lead to an apprehension of a deeper Self, which is deeply empowering. And again, Nietzsche equates the will to power with music.

But there are other things about the will to Self that also equate with music, especially as they are represented in dithyrambic drama.

High on that list is a certain mellifluence that inheres in the numerous dithyrambs that Nietzsche has written to represent the will. That mellifluence manifests itself in the various notes or movements that seem interconnected as if by a melody, insofar as the desire for Self leads to a hope for Self, which leads to a sense of Self, which leads to a vision of Self. The will to power is connected amongst its various forms, or movements, by the same thing, Self (or myth), and it is myth that makes the seemingly discordant process meaningful.

It is also important to remember that the dithyramb, as a representation of will, does not denote concept. In fact, it does not denote anything. As soon as the reader begins reading it as denotations of concepts, it makes absolutely no sense whatsoever, which should be an indication to the reader that he has gone astray, but that never happens and the reader keeps right on reading concept. The dithyramb only points, and it points to an inner state of mind, a mood, a passion, and the directives of a good conscience and, in some instances, a bad conscience. A conceptual explanation of these things would *not* result in the required isolation and delimitation that leads to embodiment of those passions in the same way that gesticulative metaphor provides clues about them that eventually lead the reader to them himself, via his own build and way, which makes it a deeper experience. Thus, what is needed to "read" a dithyramb is not conceptual thought but rather intuitive thought. In other words, one must learn to "hear" that which stirs within one self with one's own intuition, with one's own feelings and passions, because that is precisely what the gesticulative metaphors point to, your own, sometimes with very poignant detail, which is the poetry in dithyrambic music.

IN SUMMARY

Earlier in this essay, I said that at the end of every dithyramb Nietzsche wrote "Thus spoke Zarathustra." And I argued that, since the dithyramb is a literary representation of the will to power, Nietzsche could very well have written "Thus spoke the will to power" instead, and that would have been accurate. Now, we can be even more specific and say that at the end of every dithyramb, Nietzsche could have said "Thus speaks the conscience that seeks out its Self" because the will to power is also a will to Self, insofar as it is the vision of Self that empowers its beholder. And, in fact, it is the conscience, specifically the conscience that has turned bad, about which Nietzsche wrote so insightfully in *On the Genealogy of Morals* and then memorialized as poetry in many of his dithyrambs, that speaks. Again, Nietzsche's dithyrambs speak to the conscience about the conscience that only the conscience would understand. And the development of the bad conscience as a cataclysmic milestone in the history of the species as well as its healing as the fundamental and primary aim of any successful culture are two themes on which I have already elaborated extensively in The Birth of Dionysia.

But how does one address the conscience? Certainly not with concept. The conscience does not understand concept. Only the mind understands concept. On the contrary, in the same way that music does not speak to the mind but rather to your feelings, dithyrambic music also speaks to your feelings, *and only to your feelings*.

But there are no concepts explained in *Thus Spoke Zarathustra*, which does not mean you will not think conceptually. In fact, you will become highly conceptual, but the concepts you learn will come from your own experiences, not another man's explanation. That said, still, you will learn concepts, through your own experiences, that are the same concepts Nietzsche himself first spoke of. And that is the power of this new art form, the dithyramb, especially as a teacher but also as a healer.

And finally, we come to the matter of tragedy, or proto-tragedy. Proto-tragedy solves the problem that develops when myth is finally created and the "music" or the will becomes satiated and then consonant. The creation of myth condemns the will at the same time that it glorifies it and frees it. If the will cannot move past the problem that arises with mythopoeia, then the will dies and, along with it, the myth also dies. What makes tragedy so special is its ability to solve this crisis. Thus, it requires us to understand how such a phenomenon, which is critical to life, without which life is impossible and will not happen, happens. How does tragedy become a possibility and how does it actually happen?

It is also critical that the philosopher understand the birth of tragedy because it constitutes the single most fundamental question of existence: *how do the actual world of becoming and the realistic but totally illusory world of being co-exist.* There could not be two more opposed forces in all of nature, and in this instance, through the magic of tragedy, they come together and co-exist! That is the magic of tragedy!

And it is this point, the impossible genesis of tragedy, where the world of being is staunchly opposed to any destruction and the world of becoming is resolutely insistent upon it — it is this point that goes to the *nature* of the will to power and speaks most about Nietzsche's reason for referring to the text in which *Thus Spoke Zarathustra* is written as "music" or dithyrambic music.

IN SUMMARY

In the title of his *Birth of Tragedy*, Nietzsche stated that proto-tragedy happens only when a certain extreme measure of strength is first achieved. In other words, it is only when a man who is striving to apprehend the deepest and brightest vision of his Self and then finally achieves that vision that he becomes so empowered that there actually develops a need to break the tension. And the tension is caused by the extreme consonance that inheres in triumphant being. That is what Nature says, to Nietzsche and to me. Out of this extreme situation, dissonance comes into play. And dissonance is such a part of nature that one actually anticipates it and pulls it into being. Dissonance gives birth to tragedy. It is dissonance, the need for a new and deeper melody, that calls the subconscious into consciousness. (*It is all comparable to music*, this world of becoming, this will to power. It can only be understood and explained as music.) Tragedy cannot happen except as a phenomenon of music, as dissonance. Thus, its representation in the New Dithyramb might rightly be called *dithyrambic music*.

Finally, the other point to consider in order to form a concept of dithyrambic music is Nietzsche's statement that music creates myth. And to reiterate that statement, he means that dithyrambic music creates myth, though everyone continues to read it as if he is referring to audible music. In a practical sense, all it takes to understand this statement is to spend a few decades practicing his dithyrambs and living through his dithyrambic tragedy and, in the end, you will find your Self. Self is the myth that Nietzsche's dithyrambic music creates, *and it is created within you*. I know of no greater force within human nature that guides one more successfully through life than Self and conscience.

Dithyrambic drama is an extremely powerful and transformative art form. It transforms your innermost nature so that you become more natural, more functional, and more capable, in explicit defiance of what morality could ever claim to achieve, and it changes the course of your life so that it becomes more meaningful. If I have explained nothing else, I hope I have explained that.

www.ingramcontent.com/pod-product-compliance
Lightning Source LLC
Chambersburg PA
CBHW060951230426
43665CB00015B/2150